Heidegger and Happiness

Continuum Studies in Continental Philosophy
Series Editor: James Fieser, University of Tennessee at Martin, USA

Continuum Studies in Continental Philosophy is a major monograph series from Continuum. The series features first-class scholarly research monographs across the field of Continental philosophy. Each work makes a major contribution to the field of philosophical research.

Adorno's Concept of Life, Alastair Morgan
Badiou and Derrida, Antonio Calcagno
Badiou, Balibar, Ranciere, Nicholas Hewlett
Badiou, Marion and St Paul, Adam Miller
Being and Number in Heidegger's Thought, Michael Roubach
Deleuze and Guattari, Fadi Abou-Rihan
Deleuze and the Genesis of Representation, Joe Hughes
Deleuze and the Unconscious, Christian Kerslake
Deleuze, Guattari and the Production of the New, edited by Simon O'Sullivan and Stephen Zepke
Derrida, Simon Morgan Wortham
The Domestication of Derrida, Lorenzo Fabbri
Encountering Derrida, edited by Simon Morgan Wortham and Allison Weiner
Foucault's Heidegger, Timothy Rayner
Heidegger and a Metaphysics of Feeling, Sharin N. Elkholy
Heidegger and Aristotle, Michael Bowler
Heidegger and Happiness, Matthew King
Heidegger and Philosophical Atheology, Peter S. Dillard
Heidegger Beyond Deconstruction, Michael Lewis
Heidegger, Politics and Climate Change, Ruth Irwin
Heidegger's Contributions to Philosophy, Jason Powell
Heidegger's Early Philosophy, James Luchte
The Irony of Heidegger, Andrew Haas
Levinas and Camus, Tal Sessler
Merleau-Ponty's Phenomenology, Kirk M. Besmer
Nietzsche's Ethical Theory, Craig Dove
Nietzsche's Thus Spoke Zarathustra, edited by James Luchte
The Philosophy of Exaggeration, Alexander Garcia Düttmann
Ricoeur and Lacan, Karl Simms
Sartre's Phenomenology, David Reisman
Who's Afraid of Deleuze and Guattari? Gregg Lambert
Žižek and Heidegger, Thomas Brockelman

Heidegger and Happiness
Dwelling on Fitting and Being

Matthew King

continuum

Continuum International Publishing Group

The Tower Building	80 Maiden Lane
11 York Road	Suite 704
London SE1 7NX	New York NY 10038

www.continuumbooks.com

British Library Cataloguing-in-Publication Data
A catalogue record for this book is available from the British Library.

ISBN-13: PB: 978-1-4411-9129-8

Library of Congress Cataloguing-in-Publication Data
King, Matthew.
Heidegger and happiness: dwelling on fitting and being / Matthew King.
     p. cm.
  Includes bibliographical references (p.   ) and index.
  ISBN 978-1-4411-9129-8
  1. Heidegger, Martin, 1889–1976. 2. Happiness. I. Title.

  B3279.H49K499 2009
  193–dc22

                                                                    2008036326

Typeset by Newgen Imaging Systems Pvt Ltd, Chennai, India
Printed and bound in Great Britain by the MPG Books Group

Contents

Contents

Acknowledgements

Louise Gilmour helped with this book in many ways and deeply.

This book owes much to Sam Mallin, whose sensitivity to the phenomenological life in the later Heidegger was an inspiration to mine, and who finally got me to see the importance of the history of being. His 'dissertation group' also helped along the way.

The members of 'the Heidegger list' – particularly Stuart Elden, Michael Eldred, Malik Sezgin and Henk van Tuijl – offered some timely assistance.

My parents, Ruth and Robert King, made sure I had what I needed to travel the long road that has seen this book to publication. My grandparents, Stewart and Bessie Trumble, provided the cottage, which gave me the earliest experiences of deep happiness I remember.

Various parts of this book benefited from being presented to audiences at meetings of the Canadian Philosophical Association, the Canadian Society for Existential and Phenomenological Theory and Culture, the Canadian Society for Continental Philosophy, the Heidegger Circle, the Ontario Philosophical Society and the Society for Phenomenology and Existential Philosophy.

I wish to thank Jim Fieser for inviting me to propose this book to Continuum, and Tom Crick at Continuum for keeping the process of bringing it to publication moving smoothly.

Some material in Chapter 2 originally appeared in 'Heidegger's etymological method: discovering being by recovering the richness of the word', *Philosophy Today* 51, no. 3 (Fall 2007).

Acknowledgement is due to the copyright-holders for Robert Frost's 'The tuft of flowers', as follows:

Excerpts from 'The tuft of flowers' from *The Poetry of Robert Frost*, edited by Edward Connery Lathem. Copyright 1934, 1969 by Henry Holt and Company. Copyright 1962 by Robert Frost. Reprinted by permission of Henry Holt and Company, LLC.

Excerpts from 'The tuft of flowers' from *The Poetry of Robert Frost*, edited by Edward Connery Lathem, published by Jonathan Cape (1971). Reprinted by permission of Random House Group Ltd.

Introduction

Why Heidegger and Happiness?

Philosophers concerned with happiness typically want to say *what* happiness *is*. Their concern is with its *Was-sein*, its 'what-being', to use a term of Heidegger's.[1] Heidegger identifies the bifurcation of being into 'what-being' and 'that-being', starting with Plato, as philosophy's definitive starting point. After this 'event in the history of being', *that* something is is taken for granted; the concern of philosophers – and of everyone else in the Western metaphysical culture of thinking – is to know *what* it is.[2] With Plato, we want to know the thing's *essence*, its *form*, its *idea*. Any time we ask a question of the form 'what is x?', we venture into metaphysics. The essence of philosophy lies in asking 'what is x?'; that is the path that philosophy was set on by Plato, whose project centrally concerned the questions 'what is justice?', 'what is virtue?', 'what is beauty?', 'what is knowledge?' and so on.

My project in this book is not to better define the sense of 'happiness' or to describe the form of the various phenomena called happiness. But it is related to projects such as those, in that it aims to bring to light an aspect of happiness which is, if not usually overlooked, then usually described inadequately in the philosophical terms marshalled to the task. I will call this aspect 'deep' happiness, because in my view it is the most important and characteristically human kind of happiness there is. This kind of happiness has to do with the role of human being in the happening of being. As Heidegger maintains, Western thinking since its inception in ancient Greece has been oblivious of the happening of being. This oblivion accounts for the inadequacy of any attempts hitherto to describe deep happiness. I hope to show in this book that just as Heidegger's thinking towards overcoming the oblivion of being can help us to understand deep happiness, deep happiness can be a key to overcoming the oblivion of being. Through this reciprocal illumination, especially with the aid of sketches (which may be called 'phenomenological' in a sense appropriate to the later Heidegger's thinking) of some experiences of deep happiness, I hope to show that what Heidegger is trying to show us through his thinking concerning being is not so removed from ordinary experience as it is too often taken to be.

I fear that I may have already given readers who are not intimately familiar with Heidegger cause to doubt the last point with the opaque and strange-sounding formulations in the last paragraph. More concepts derived directly or indirectly from Heidegger will be introduced without much explanation in this section. This is necessary to get the issues I will be dealing with on the table, and it may be frustrating or aggravating at first. But one of my aims in this book, which can only be pursued gradually and by continually returning again and again to experience and to the texts, is to bring out the phenomenal life in some of Heidegger's most important language, so hopefully the frustration and aggravation will not last too long.

'Heidegger and happiness' may seem an odd combination. *Angst* is famously prominent in *Being and Time*, but happiness, as such, is not a topic that occupies Heidegger's attention. His characteristically dour proclamations about 'the darkening of the world' and 'the devastation of the earth' may lead us to believe that Heidegger is not interested in such frivolous matters as happiness. In one of the few places where Heidegger mentions happiness, he writes that 'the devastation of the earth can easily go hand in hand with a guaranteed supreme living standard for man, and just as easily with the organized establishment of a uniform state of happiness [*Glückszustandes*] for all men'.[3] Later in the same work Heidegger quotes from *Thus Spoke Zarathustra*: 'The earth has become smaller, and on it hops the last man who makes everything small. His race is as ineradicable as the flea-beetle; the last man lives longest. "We have invented happiness" – say the last men, and they blink.'[4]

The kind of happiness which, Heidegger holds, can go hand in hand with 'the devastation of the earth' is the kind of happiness that 'the last men' have 'invented', which is roughly the happiness of utilitarianism, the happiness of a surplus of pleasure over pain, of comfort and security – but, as we will see, it is equally the kind of happiness that Nietzsche's *Übermenschen* will invent, the happiness of will-realization. We find these two kinds of happiness combined in a view of happiness that is common today, among philosophers and others, namely, that happiness consists in desire-satisfaction. If the happiness of desire-satisfaction were the only kind of happiness to be had, then it would be fair to say that there could be no Heideggerian philosophical use for happiness.

However, one of this book's main aims is to show that this is an incomplete and impoverished view of happiness. Happiness, I will urge, in its deepest sense, consists in being as it is fitting for human beings to be, and this in turn consists in dwelling in our fitting-together with being – and these matters are at the heart of Heidegger's thought throughout his career, but especially after the so-called 'turn' in his thinking after the publication of *Being and Time*.[5] As I will try to show in Chapter 2, Heidegger's enduring, essential insight is that being *happens*. Though the happening of being is understood very differently on either side of the 'turn', the happening of being is always understood to be intimately related to human being. Before the 'turn', Heidegger understands being as a *temporal* happening. This understanding of being begins with the temporality of our own being, which can begin to be revealed to us in moments of 'authenticity', *Eigentlichkeit*. In these moments we take responsibility for the direction of our own lives, detaching ourselves from the 'one-size-fits-all' mode of existence that is prepared for us by the milieu in which we live, and forging for ourselves a way of life that is fitting for us as the particular human beings we are, individuated by the prospect of our own unique deaths.

This kind of fittingness having to do with 'authenticity' will not play an important role in the development of my notion of deep happiness in this book. The importance of authenticity for Heidegger's philosophy in *Being and Time* has been greatly exaggerated – authenticity is a station along the way to the discovery of the temporal meaning of being; it is not an end in itself. Moreover, the idea of the fitting life as a *self-willed* project is the kind of idea that Heidegger will come to reject through his self-critical engagement with Nietzsche in the mid-to-late 1930s. The idea that one must *will* a fitting life for oneself is part and parcel of the latest 'epoch' in the 'history of being', which the later Heidegger identifies as the most dangerous yet for our dwelling in our fitting together with being.

Heidegger's later work provides what I take to be the richest resources for understanding how it is fitting for human beings to be – and his later work has always resonated with my own notions of what human happiness is, for reasons which I only dimly apprehended in my first, uncertain approaches to Heidegger's thinking, but which will hopefully become clear over the course of this book. On my interpretation, in his later work, Heidegger comes to understand being as a *happening-to-us*. This, I propose, is the essential meaning of Heidegger's term *Ereignis*, which guides his thought after the 'turn'. The being of things happens through its fitting-together with us, and our own being happens through its fitting-together with the being of things. Being happens to us; by contrast, it does not happen to, for instance, computers, and while it may happen to non-human animals, only human beings are able to dwell in and respond to its happening.

This happening does not happen once, or on occasion, or intermittently. It happens all the time, though we hardly ever pay attention to it. In the grip of philosophical ideologies, we even deny the phenomenon of its happening. Among the more practically dangerous manifestations of this denial is the denial that there is any difference between our relation with things and that of a robot equipped with sensors for detecting and responding to physical events.[6] But we – we Westerners immersed in the metaphysical tradition of thought, especially in the current technological epoch – fail to recognize being's happening to us, denying that being happens at all. The whole purpose of Heidegger's later work is to prepare us to see that being happens, to dwell in and affirm its happening and our essential place in its happening. It is my thesis that the most profound human happiness consists in our dwelling in this fitting-together of human being and the being of beings, this fitting-together in which being is fulfilled in its reception by human being and in which human being is fulfilled by being's happening to it.

Heidegger almost always seems determined to resist 'application' of his work, from his insistence in *Being and Time* that what he says there 'has a purely ontological intention and is far removed from any moralizing critique of everyday *Da-sein*',[7] to his admonition in *An Introduction to Metaphysics* that 'it is absolutely correct and proper to say that "You can't do anything with philosophy," '[8] to his declaration in the *Spiegel* interview that philosophy is powerless to save us from the 'absolute technological state' (and that only a god could do that).[9] And yet Medard Boss reports that Heidegger told him that he had chosen to collaborate with him because 'he had hoped that through me – a physician and psychotherapist – his thinking would escape the confines of the philosopher's study and become of benefit to wider circles, in particular to a large number of suffering human beings'.[10] We cannot say for certain exactly what Heidegger might have meant by this; the protocols of Heidegger's Zollikon Seminars, hosted by Boss and attended by Boss's psychiatric colleagues, reveal little on this question, preoccupied as they are with abstract matters pertaining to Heidegger's earlier thought. Nonetheless, it seems clear that, in Heidegger's view, our oblivion of being, which has reached a peak in the current technological epoch, is a disaster for human well-being in the deepest sense, and that we will be better off – we will be more at home in ourselves; we will be more fittingly – if and when the epoch turns such that the oblivion of being is overcome. Perhaps we cannot *will* that turning; perhaps we cannot even will it for our own lives, let alone for the epochal relationship between being and human being. But we can catch a glimpse of it. Indeed, if we could not, it could never come about at all – and to catch a glimpse of it is already to begin the turning.

The rest of this Introduction will sketch out, first, the two senses in which the later Heidegger speaks of being, second, the senses of fitting and dwelling with which this book is concerned, and third, three different schemes of affective states that Heidegger devises at three different points in his career. This will lay the groundwork for the development of my conception of deep happiness as consisting in our dwelling in our fitting together with being, and my thesis that the affective state of deep happiness can afford us a particular insight into being. The book's four chapters will develop that conception as follows. First, I will engage with the history of thought on happiness, showing how, at the beginning of that history, happiness was strongly associated with fittingness. Second, I will elaborate Heidegger's later thinking on being, paying particular attention to the role language plays in presenting being to us, and making an etymological case that a sense of fittingness is embedded in the word 'happiness'. Third, I will explore the later Heidegger's thinking concerning the human essence and the way being happens in the fitting-together of 'mortals' with 'earth', 'sky' and 'divinities'. Fourth, I will place my notion of deep happiness in the context of Heidegger's 'history of being', showing how we might get closer to deep happiness by moving back through the 'epochs' of being.

The Later Heidegger's Two Senses of 'Being'

There is an important sense in which we find Heidegger speaking explicitly about a 'fitting', *schicklich*, relation between human being and being. However, it is not the sense of fitting-together between human being and being in which I propose deep happiness consists, because different senses of being are at issue. Understanding the difference between these two different senses of being is crucial to the elucidation of my conception of human being's fitting together with being and Heidegger's later thinking about being and *Ereignis*. I will sketch out the difference here; it will be elaborated over the course of this book.

In the 'Letter on "humanism"', Heidegger writes:

For humans the question ever remains whether they find what is fitting [*schicklich*] in their essence, which corresponds [*entspricht*] with [the] destining [*Geschick*] [of being]; for in accordance with this they have, as those who ek-sist, to guard the truth of being. The human being is the shepherd of being.[11]

What does it mean to 'guard the truth of being', to be 'the shepherd of being'? At issue here is the role of human being in the succession of epochs which, for Heidegger, constitute the history of being. Heidegger writes that 'the human being is "thrown" by being itself into the truth of being'. 'Truth', for Heidegger, always refers to ἀλήθεια, as he interprets that Greek word, that is, as 'unconcealment'; thus human beings are thrown by being itself into (or in other words, we find ourselves always already related to) the unconcealment (or, put positively, the self-revealing) of being.

The phrase 'thrown by being itself' risks the interpretation that 'being itself' is some God-like *thing*, an agency which intentionally acts on us, which 'decides' to throw us. That risk is compounded by the possibility that we will take the talk of 'destiny' to mean that something like 'God's plan' is behind the history of being. Such an interpretation gives credence to, as it is also lent credence by, the view that Heidegger is a mystic or a poet-metaphysician. But such an interpretation ignores Heidegger's enduring phenomenological approach; it takes what he is saying as speculative *explanation* rather than *description*. To say that we are 'thrown' by being means that being is always already *happening to us* in some *way* or other. The *ways* in which being happens to us differ in different epochs. When Heidegger speaks of the 'destining' of being he emphasizes the root *schicken*, meaning 'to send'. We ought to hear 'destining' as moving towards a destination: human beings are a, if not the, destination of being, not in the sense that being deliberately sets out to reach us, but in the sense that when being does reach us, it has arrived at its home, so to speak. Thus the history of being consists in the different ways that being is *sent* to us in different epochs (as we will see in more detail in Chapter 4).

The task of human beings, to 'find what is fitting in their essence, which corresponds with the destining of being', is carried out above all by those whom Heidegger calls 'essential thinkers', figures such as Plato, Aristotle, Descartes and Nietzsche, who are typically considered to have founded paradigms of metaphysical thought. These are the thinkers who find the fitting description of the way that being is sent to us in a given epoch; essential thinkers are the ones who, more than all others, 'respond', *entsprechen*, to the call, *Geheiß*, that they hear, *hören*, in their belonging, *Gehören*, to being. Commenting on his characterization of Nietzsche as an essential thinker, Heidegger says: 'With the term *thinker* we name those exceptional human beings who are destined to think one single thought, a thought that is always "about" *beings as a* whole'[12] – that is, it is a *metaphysical* thought; for Heidegger, metaphysics is precisely defined as 'inquiry beyond or over beings that aims to recover them as such and as a whole for our grasp'.[13] Since it is the thought of *the way being is now*, it is, in principle, available for all to think; the distinction of the thinker is to be the one who first finds the fitting words to describe it. In another lecture, but again in reference to Nietzsche and the proposition that 'every thinker thinks one single thought', Heidegger writes that 'for the thinker the difficulty is to hold fast to this single thought as the one and only thing that he must think; to think this One as the Same; and to tell of this Same in the fitting [*gemäße*] manner'.[14] To think this one as the same: the single thought is the thought of that which is the same about *everything* that is, *insofar* as it is; it is the thought of beings *as such* and *as a whole* – for Plato, the thought that everything that is, insofar as it is, is an ἰδέα; for Nietzsche, the thought that everything that is, insofar as it is, is will to power. In thinking the currently dominant epoch that Heidegger calls *Ge-Stell* – a word that means 'frame' and, in Heidegger's use, can be glossed as the enframing technological besetting of things – Heidegger stands in the place of the thinker, but, as we will see in Chapter 4, the thought of *Ge-Stell* is essentially Nietzsche's; the epoch of *Ge-Stell* is an intensification of the epoch of will to power, or as Heidegger puts it, will to will.

Heidegger derives his word 'epoch' from the word ἐποχή, a word familiar from Husserlian phenomenology that is commonly rendered in English as 'bracketing'. Heidegger identifies its meaning as 'to hold back', *'an sich halten'*.[15] The significance of the word 'epoch' as Heidegger uses it is that each epoch of being is both a way of presencing, *Anwesenheit*, and a holding back, *an sich halten*. We might say that there is a threefold holding back in any epoch of being. First, other possible ways of presencing are held back. Second, the given way of presencing is only one way of presencing is held back. Third, the very presencing itself, the happening-to-us, of being, is held back.

The third holding-back has to do with the later Heidegger's particular thought, which is more fundamental than that of the 'essential thinker': the essential thinker brings to words the way that being happens, but what Heidegger most profoundly brings to words is *that* being happens at all. Being in its happening-to-us is the most important – for our purposes, and for Heidegger as well – of the later Heidegger's two senses of being. It is being in this sense that Heidegger tries to mark as different from being as it has been conceived through the history of metaphysics by using such devices as the archaic spelling *Seyn* instead of *Sein* and placing a cross through the word *Sein*. It is being in this sense that Heidegger describes as *Ereignis*, which is the German word for 'event', though Heidegger's meaning is perhaps better captured by 'happening': being is a happening, a taking-place, that occurs in the mutual *appropriation* (which is the most usual translation of Heidegger's *Ereignis*, for reasons I will examine) of human being and being. In this sense of 'being', Heidegger can write in the *Contributions to Philosophy* that '*Seyn* is *Er-eignis*'.[16] On the other hand, where being in the sense of epochal destining is concerned (and Heidegger always writes *Sein* for being in this sense), Heidegger says that 'thinking must . . . overcome the habit of yielding to the view that we are thinking . . . of "being" as *Ereignis*. . . . *Ereignis* is essentially different, because it is richer than any possible metaphysical determination of being. Being, however, in respect of its essential origin, can be thought of in terms of *Ereignis*'.[17] With the two senses of being in mind, using *Seyn* for being in the sense of being's happening to us and *Sein* for being in the sense of the way it is sent to us in a given epoch, we can interpret the latter statement as follows: *Seyn* is essentially other than *Sein*, because it is richer than any possible determination of *Sein*. *Sein*, however, in respect of its essential origin, can be thought of in terms of *Seyn*. *Seyn* is, not the well, but the wellspring, not the sender, but the very sending, the coming to presence, the happening to us, which manifests itself in *Sein*. *Seyn* is being as happening-to-us; *Sein* is being as the way in which the happening of *Seyn* happens to us.[18]

We find the difference between *Seyn* and *Sein* laid out in the following passage from the *Gesamtausgabe* version of Heidegger's lecture 'The turning': 'The human *essence* belongs to the essence of *Seyn* – inasmuch as *Seyn*'s essence needs man's essence, in order to remain kept safe [*gewahrt*] as *Sein* in keeping with its own essence in the midst of beings, and thus to essence as *Seyn*.'[19] With the word *gewahrt*, Heidegger plays, as he often does, on the common roots of *wahren*, to keep, and *Wahrheit*, truth. Thus we may understand this passage as follows: *Seyn* is 'kept safe' – that is, its happening is allowed for – by the human essence (which I will examine in Chapter 3) through its coming to truth, which for Heidegger means unconcealing itself, as *Sein*, that is, as a particular epochal way of being. 'In the midst of beings' indicates that *Sein*, in turn, always presents itself as *das Sein des Seiende*, the being of beings. This relation between *Sein* and *das Sein des Seiendes* is indicated in the following passage in 'The onto-theo-logical constitution of metaphysics': 'The being of beings means being which is beings. The "is" here speaks transitively, in transition. . . . Being transits [*geht über*, goes over/across] (that), comes unconcealingly over (that) which arrives as something of itself unconcealed only by that coming-over [*Überkommnis*].'[20] Being in the sense of a particular epochal way-of-being 'comes across' through beings, determining them in their being.

We may summarize the two senses of 'being' in the later Heidegger as follows. First, there is being in its deepest sense, which we may call being per se, the sense of happening-to-us. This is the sense that Heidegger some-times renders as *Seyn* and sometimes as ~~being~~, and which is described as *Ereignis*. Second, there is being in the sense of the epochal way-of-being. To think being in the second sense is the task of those Heidegger calls 'essential thinkers'; to think being in the first sense is Heidegger's own unique task.

Fitting and Dwelling

The concept of fitting figures centrally in the earliest surviving pas-sage attributed to a Western philosopher. In a fragment passed down by Simplicius, Anaximander is reported to have said (as a typical translation has it): 'the things that are perish into the things out of which they come to be, according to necessity, for they pay penalty [δίκην] and retribution to each other for their injustice [ἀδικίας] in accordance with the ordering of time'.[21] Heidegger discusses this fragment in two works, first in the final part of the 1941 lecture course translated as *Basic Concepts*, and again in the longer 1946 essay 'The Anaximander fragment'. In both pieces, Heidegger rejects the standard German translations (by Nietzsche and Diels) of δίκην and ἀδικίας as *Buße* (penalty) and *Ungerechtigkeiten* (Nietzsche's word, meaning injustices) or *Ruchlosigkeit* (Diels's word, meaning nefariousness). Heidegger translates δίκην instead with the German word *Fug* and ἀδικίας with *Unfug*. The former is archaic, but the latter, which means 'disorder' or 'mischief', is still in use in contemporary German. Aylesworth's translation of *Basic Concepts* renders *Fug* as 'fit'; the two English translations of 'The Anaximander fragment' render it as 'order'.[22] Though the latter preserves the contrast with the usual translations of *Unfug*, 'fit' brings out more of the sense of the German word, as it shows its relation to *Fuge*, joint, and *fügen*, to join. At any rate, order is derivative of fit, since that which is ordered is that in which everything has its fitting place. Indeed, Liddell and Scott define δίκη in one of its senses as 'order' or 'right', and give the following example: 'μή τι δίκης ἐπιδευές' – 'nothing short of *what is fit*'.[23]

Heidegger prefers *Fug* to words having to do with 'justice' in the jurid-ical sense because the latter lend themselves to the common interpretation that 'in this fragment a "physical law of the universe" is expressed "in eth-ical and juridical notions"' – but 'at that time there was no physics and therefore no physical thinking . . ., no jurisprudence and therefore no jur-idical thinking'.[24] In other words, Anaximander is not speaking metaphor-ically, not drawing an analogy; he is not forced, by a lack of appropriate 'scientific' terms, to apply juridical terms to physics. Rather, the original sense of δίκη – which is also the root of δικαιοσύνη, the name of the virtue rendered as 'justice' in translations of Plato and Aristotle, which, as we will see in Chapter 1, is in Plato's thought intimately related to happiness or εὐδαιμονία as kinds of fittingness – encompasses both of what would come to be specified as the juridical and the physical. In that original sense, it means simply the fitting.

If δίκη indeed means the fitting, then the Anaximander fragment has the following sense: that which is comes to be and passes away as is fitting; that which is fits where and when it is, and when it no longer fits, it no longer is. For my purposes here we need not be concerned with what Anaximander might have thought it means for things to fit. What is essential is this: not only has Western philosophy been centrally concerned with the idea of fitting from its very beginnings, but from its very beginnings it has conceived of *being* in terms of fitting.

What is fitting? What does it mean to fit? 'Fitting' in the first place normally refers to relations between physical things, and there are two different but related senses in which we ordinarily speak of physical things *fitting*, which we may call *fitting-in* and *fitting-together*. In the sense of fitting-in, we say of things that they fit when they do not exceed the space allotted to them, and especially when they just fill it: the clothes fit in the suitcase, the boxes fit in the car. In the sense of fitting-together, we say of things that they fit when they join together snugly, often to fulfil a certain end. This is the sense in which two jigsaw puzzle pieces or two gears fit together, and in which a 'fitting' is used to fit two pipes together. Fitting-in and fitting-together are closely related, as demonstrated by the fact that we can say either that a hand fits in a glove or that a glove and hand fit together; similarly, the puzzle pieces fit together because a bit of one just fills a space in the other.

The more 'metaphorical' kinds of 'fitting' with which I am concerned in this book are related to each of these two senses in which physical things are said to fit. Corresponding to the sense of fitting-in, we can ascribe fittingness to our lives (or elements of them, such as our careers, our family arrangements, or our desires and aspirations) when our lives are somehow appropriate to us. Fitting-in, when applied to the shapes of human lives, can be described as fitting-for. My life may be fitting for me either as a specific individual or as a human being in general. For example, I, as a specific individual, may or may not be fit for the life of a philosopher: there is a certain shape to that life which I must approximately fill out and not exceed, and if I lack the capabilities to do so, then it is not a fitting life for me. But it also may or may not be fitting for human beings in general to philosophize, or, conversely, to live without philosophizing. It is the latter kind of fitting-in, the kind having to do with what is fitting for human beings in general, which will be at issue in this book.

The most important sense of fitting for my purposes, however, is fitting-together. In the last section, I said that the later Heidegger understands being itself as a happening-to-us. When the being of things happens to us (and it is happening to us all the time), we can be said to fit together with being: being is 'toward' us; we have capacities to receive being; the happening of being, *Ereignis*, occurs when being fits together with our capacities to receive being. What is most fitting for us is to dwell in our fitting together with being.

The concept of fitting is closely related to that of dwelling. When we fit in, we say that we are at home. Throughout his career, Heidegger is concerned with the notions of being at home and dwelling, and his treatment of these notions is remarkably similar in his earlier and later thinking. The possibility of being at home or not at home, or more generally of being in place or out of place in a certain sense, is always for Heidegger distinctive of human beings.[25] This is because only human beings *have* a place (again, in a certain sense), and this in turn is because only human being consists of being-in-the-world, in the sense Heidegger gives to that phrase in *Being and Time*. Of course, other types of things can be out of place, in other senses. For instance, we can speak of a rock being out of place. A basalt boulder carried out of the Canadian Shield by a glacier and brought to rest above the limestone of southern Ontario is, in a sense, out of place. It is out of place in the sense that it has been removed from the place where it was formed, and carried to a place where there are no, or very few, other things like it – it 'stands out', it does not fit in with its surroundings.

But this is not the way of being out of place that belongs to human being. The boulder *is* in a place, but a human being, unlike a boulder, *has* its place. Heidegger explains the difference between the sense in which things like boulders are in the world, and the sense of being-in-the-world which is essential to human being, as follows. On one hand, when we say that 'objectively present' (*vorhanden*) things are 'in' the world, 'by this "in" we mean the relation of being that two beings extended "in" space have to each other with regard to their location in that space'.[26] On the other hand, human being-in-the-world does not 'designate a spatial "in one another" of two things objectively present', but rather means to 'dwell' in the world and 'take care of' it.[27] That we 'dwell' in the world means that our being *goes out into* the world, that it is *involved with* things in the world. To 'take care of the world' means to take it *into* our care. In dwelling and taking care, human being becomes intermingled with the being of 'objectively present' beings, which the latter do not do with each other. This is why Heidegger says that 'two beings which are objectively present within the world . . . can never "touch" each other'.[28] To 'touch', as human beings touch, does not mean merely to be contiguous with another thing, but rather to *take in* the being of the contiguous thing.[29] To touch as human beings touch is to *feel*, to be *affected* by the being of another being; this is why, as Heidegger points out, our experience is essentially affective, and not merely 'coloured' by affective states.[30] Moreover, this is why the way a human being relates to things is fundamentally different from the way an information-processing machine relates to things: the information-processing machine touches without feeling, it is moved without being affected. The machine does not receive the being of what it processes.

What does it mean, then, for human beings to be out of place? The 'feeling' of being out of place, of strangeness, is in German called *Unheimlichkeit*, literally not-at-home-ness, usually translated in Heidegger's works as 'uncanniness'. This feeling plays an important role in the project of *Being and Time*. The main discussion of it in *Being and Time* takes place in the section on *Angst*. 'In *Angst*', Heidegger writes, 'one has an "*unheimlich*" feeling'.[31] In *Angst* one *feels* one's *Unheimlichkeit*, the tension between one's 'lostness' in the indefiniteness of *das Man*, the 'they', and one's subterranean sense of the finitude of one's own life. Heidegger points out that 'lostness' in *das Man* ordinarily is not *felt* as lostness, but rather as its own kind of 'being-at-home': 'the everyday publicness of *das Man* . . . brings tranquillized self-assurance, "being-at-home" with all its obviousness, into the average everydayness of *Da-sein*'.[32]

Conformity with *das Man* is a kind of fitting – we commonly call it 'fitting in'. When we fit in with *das Man*, willingly doing 'what is done' because it is 'what is done' rather than choosing our possibilities for ourselves, Heidegger says we are 'tranquillized'. The 'tranquillization' found in fitting in with *das Man*, though widely deplored in our superficially individualist culture, often seems to us to amount to a kind of happiness. In this tranquillized fitting-in indeed we do not consciously want our lives to go differently. Certainly the failure to fit in is felt by many as a source of unhappiness. But for Heidegger, this kind of 'being-at-home' is shallow if not false (as indicated by his scare quotes around the phrase in the passage quoted at the end of the last paragraph). Most importantly for Heidegger's purposes, it diverts us from the possibility of developing an ontological understanding of being, because it obscures our *Unheimlichkeit*: 'Entangled flight *into* the being-at-home of publicness is flight *from* not-being-at-home, that is, from the *Unheimlichkeit* which lies in *Da-sein* as thrown.'[33] However, Heidegger continues, 'this *Unheimlichkeit* constantly pursues *Da-sein* and threatens its everyday lostness in the they'. When our *Unheimlichkeit* catches up with us, it manifests itself as the 'uncanny', strange feeling of 'not being oneself' – the feeling that the life one is living is not one's own, and that one is losing the possibilities that one might choose for oneself in living one's own life. This feeling or 'mood' (*Stimmung*) marks the attunement (*Befindlichkeit*) of *Angst*, and it prepares us for the possibility of 'authenticity', *Eigentlichkeit* – the state of being one's own self. In moments of authenticity, when we own up to the finite possibilities in our futures, we gain an insight into the temporality our existence, which is the key to the possibility of our understanding being itself in its temporal happening.

The main source for Heidegger's later thinking concerning dwelling is the 1951 lecture 'Building dwelling thinking'. There Heidegger says that the fundamental sense of dwelling is 'sparing' or 'preserving', *Schonen*, and to spare is to 'guard' or 'take care of', *hüten*.[34] In the sense of dwelling that Heidegger develops, we can be said most properly to dwell in our taking care of, our attending to, the happening to us of being.[35] 'Dwelling is the manner in which mortals are on the earth'[36] – but we are not always, or even usually, ourselves as mortals, nor on the earth as earth. Though we are always fitting together with being, we are not always or even usually dwelling. But this is not necessarily a bad thing, from the perspective of thinking about being. In his 1942 lecture-course on Hölderlin's *Der Ister*, Heidegger emphasizes that to be truly at home is to return from a foreign land; the home-y-ness of home is not apparent to us unless we have been away from home.[37] As beings that fit together with being, we are at home in being, and we 'dwell' in taking being into our care. But this dwelling is something that we can dwell *on*, that we can pause to reflect on, when we come to dwelling in being after having failed to dwell. The experiences of deep happiness that I will sketch from time to time in this book are all experiences of returning home to being, of returning to dwell in fitting together with being. In such experiences, we have the opportunity to see what we have been missing, what Heidegger says we have been missing since the dawn of Western thought: the happening-to-us of being.

Heidegger's Schemes of Affective States

Throughout his career, Heidegger remains concerned with the role of affective states in our reception of being, and with differentiating between different kinds of affective states. It will be helpful for us, then, to lay out the schemes of affective states that he devises at various points, to provide some conceptual framework that will help us to understand the role that happiness, in the sense I am developing, plays in our reception of being.

I will focus on three texts originating from what can be called Heidegger's early, middle and late periods: before the 'turn', in the midst of it, and after it. The first text is *Being and Time*, the second is the first volume of the *Nietzsche* lectures, and the third is the 1955 lecture *What is Philosophy?* In both *Being and Time* and *What is Philosophy?*, Heidegger is concerned with the relationship between affective states and our connection with being. In *Nietzsche I*, the analysis of affective states is undertaken to help in understanding the significance of the 'will to power'. Hence we will find similarities between the accounts in *Being and Time* and *What is Philosophy?*, even though they are texts from either side of the 'turn' in Heidegger's thinking, which we will not find between either of them and *Nietzsche I*. Despite the differences between the three texts, however, in the end there will emerge a fairly coherent picture of Heidegger's basic view on affective states and their role in our understanding of the temporal happening of being (for the early Heidegger) or being's happening to us (for the later Heidegger).

Being and Time: *Befindlichkeit* and *Stimmung*

Two terms for kinds of affective states are prominent in *Being and Time*, namely, *Befindlichkeit* and *Stimmung*. The translations by Macquarrie and Robinson and by Stambaugh both render the latter as 'mood'; the former Macquarrie and Robinson render as 'state-of-mind' and Stambaugh as 'attunement'.[38] Both translations of *Befindlichkeit* are problematic, 'state-of-mind' (as has been widely noted by commentators) because of its psychologistic implications and 'attunement' because the meaning of this and related words having to do with 'tuning' is actually closer to that of *Stimmung* and related words like *Gestimmtheit* and *Bestimmtheit* – in fact, translators of other works (e.g. the *Contributions to Philosophy*) sometimes render *Stimmung* as 'attunement'. Hubert Dreyfus, meanwhile, noting that the German expression '*Wie befinden Sie sich?*' is equivalent to the colloquial English 'how are you doing?', writes that he had tried 'disposition', 'situatedness' and 'where-you're-at-ness' as translations of *Befindlichkeit*, before settling on 'affectedness'.[39] I will adopt Dreyfus's word, since I am calling what I am concerned with here 'affective states', enquiring as to what sort of affective state deep happiness might be.[40]

The translation of *Stimmung* with 'mood' may be somewhat unhappy as well, both in that 'mood' cannot be modified easily to accommodate the words related to *Stimmung*, and in that (unlike 'attunement') it may be susceptible to the same kind of psychologistic misreadings as 'state-of-mind'. However, rendering *Stimmung* as 'mood' has the advantage of indicating that *Stimmung* is not something unfamiliar, something removed from the way we ordinarily experience and describe our affective states. Moreover, the difference between our usual psychologistic assumptions about mood and Heidegger's view of *Stimmung* does not necessarily indicate that Heidegger's *Stimmung* does not name the same phenomena that we name with mood; it may rather be (and I propose that it is) the case that the way we think of moods needs to be corrected in light of what Heidegger says about *Stimmung*. *Das Gestimmtsein*, being-mooded, Heidegger writes, 'is not initially related to something psychical, it is not itself an inner condition which then in some mysterious way reaches out and leaves its mark on things and persons', because '*mood has always already disclosed being-in-the-world as a whole and first makes possible directing oneself toward something*'.[41] The mood that one is in is not independent of one's experience of the world; it is rather constitutive of the way one experiences things. One cannot 'overcome' a mood to examine one's experience free of affective 'colour'; 'the purest *theōria* does not abandon all moods' but approaches its objects in a 'tranquil' mood.[42] These claims of Heidegger's have real critical impact when we consider them as pertaining to what we actually call 'moods', an impact which they would lose if we supposed that *Stimmung* named some more esoteric state.

What, then, is the difference between *Befindlichkeit* and *Stimmung*, between affectedness and mood? The widespread disagreement about how to translate *Befindlichkeit*, and the fact that the same word has been used to translate both *Befindlichkeit* and *Stimmung*, may be an indication of how difficult it is to distinguish between the two concepts.[43] On Heidegger's scheme, affectedness is the name of the ontological structures indicated by the ontic phenomena of mood, where the term 'ontological' refers to the structures which allow for our relation with being, and the term 'ontic' refers to the manifestation of those structures in actual beings. Affectedness names the fact that our relation to being is affectively determined somehow or other; mood is the name for the particular affective states which determine that relation. The mood of *Unheimlichkeit* is an ontic manifestation of the way of being affected called *Angst*.[44] This is why it may be preferable to leave *Angst* untranslated, as Stambaugh does, instead of translating it as 'anxiety'. Anxiety is familiar to us as an affective state – we *feel* anxious, we are in an anxious *mood*.[45] But *Angst*, as a way of being affected, is not something that we experience directly. Being-apprehensive-of-my-end (which I would venture as the best gloss of *Angst*) is something that is always with us, not in the sense that it lurks in an 'unconscious', but in that it is always partially determinative of our relationship with the world. A *Befindlichkeit* is not a phenomenon itself, but is present *in* phenomena (particularly, in a mood), and it is the task of hermeneutic phenomenology to discern and describe it.[46]

In the context of his explication of mood, Heidegger mentions another kind of affective state, namely, 'being affected', *Affektion* or *Betroffenheit*. To be affected in the sense invoked with these words seems to be to have what we would ordinarily call an affect, or in other words a 'feeling' in the sense that happiness is usually thought to be a feeling. Heidegger's main concern regarding affects is to point out that they are grounded in affectedness, that affectedness makes it possible to have affects:

> being affected . . . is ontologically possible only because being-in as such is existentially determined beforehand in such a way that what it encounters in the world can *matter* to it in this way. This mattering to it is grounded in affectedness, and as affectedness it has disclosed the world, for example, as something by which it can be threatened.[47]

This speaks to the point that affectedness is not something distinct from, 'added onto' or caused by, our experience of the world. A frightening experience can make one have the affect of feeling frightened only because *Angst* is one of *Da-Sein*'s ways of being affected.

Hence there are, in *Being and Time*, three 'layers' of affective states which may be summarized as follows. First, our being-in-the-world is made possible by its affectedness or ways of being affected. *Angst* is one of the ways – for *Being and Time*, the most important way – in which we are affected. Second, our ways of being affected manifest themselves in moods, which are the particular affective states that 'attune' our experience of things. What Heidegger calls *Unheimlichkeit*, what we are familiar with as 'edginess' or 'anxiety' in the most ordinary sense, are moods that can manifest *Angst* most evidently. Finally, our ways of being affected are also revealed in the particular affects or 'feelings' which they allow us to have.

What, then, of happiness? The common 'utilitarian' conception has it that happiness is a feeling or a mood. Heidegger gives us an unusual way of thinking about feelings and moods: they reveal a deeper kind of affective state, which we are calling our ways of being affected. Moreover, moods, if not feelings, are constitutive of our experience of the world. On the later-Heideggerian understanding of being, to say that moods are constitutive of our experience of the world is to say that moods (partially) determine how being happens to us – moods determine how we *fit together* with being.

We may want to ask whether deep happiness is particularly suited to reveal to us a certain way of being affected, as 'uncanniness' is particularly suited to reveal *Angst. Angst*, being-apprehensive-of-my-end, is for *Being and Time* the most important of our ways of being affected because it is the source of our pre-ontological understanding of temporality, which is supposed to be the key to our coming to an ontological understanding of being. Heidegger, in *Being and Time*, thinks that *Angst* reveals something, the most important thing, about being. I am working on the view that *happiness* is the affective state which relates to being in the most profound way. My view, however, is that we are most profoundly related to being *when we are happy*, and this is not consistent with the view that happiness is a way of being affected that is always with us, even when we feel very unhappy. In any event, soon after *Being and Time*, Heidegger drops the distinction between *Befindlichkeit* and *Stimmung*, along with the distinction between the ontic and the ontological on which it rests.[48] I will turn now to see what Heidegger has to tell us about affective states once this distinction has been effaced.

Nietzsche I: *Affekt, Leidenschaft* and *Gefühl*

Early in the first volume of the *Nietzsche* lectures, Heidegger devotes a chapter to the relationship between affective states and the will to power. Noting that Nietzsche sometimes characterizes will as affect (*Affekt*) and sometimes as passion (*Leidenschaft*), Heidegger sets out to analyse these two concepts, using anger and hatred as examples of an affect and a passion, respectively. Anger is an affect in that it affects us; 'we cannot plan or decide to be angry', but rather anger 'comes over us, seizes us'.[49] However, hate also 'cannot be produced by a decision'.[50] The difference is that hate is 'nurtured' in us and does not 'blow over' like anger.[51] Anger may be thought here to be the germ of hate (Heidegger also briefly invokes infatuation and love as examples of an affect and a passion), but the difference between them is not only that between the shorter and longer term. An affect and a passion structure our experience of ourselves and of the world differently. Whereas in anger 'something stirs us up, lifts us beyond ourselves, . . . in such a way that . . . we are no longer master of ourselves',[52] hate 'gathers our essential being to its proper [*eigentlich*] ground . . . so that the passion is that through which and in which we take hold of ourselves and achieve perspicuous mastery over the beings around us and within us'.[53]

Heidegger summarizes the difference this way: 'Affect: the seizure that blindly agitates us. Passion: the lucidly gathering grip on beings'.[54]

Affects and passions both draw us out from ourselves into an involvement with beings, but that involvement is unreflective in the case of affects and reflective in the case of passions. Like moods on the terms of *Being and Time*, affects and passions do not occur only now and then; it is not the case that sometimes I have an affect and sometimes a passion, sometimes both and sometimes neither. Passions, given their subterranean nurturance, are always with us. So, too, are affects: just as Heidegger writes in *Being and Time* that 'the often persistent, smooth, and pallid lack of mood' is also a mood,[55] so too what is commonly known as 'flat affect' – which is perhaps identical with, and perhaps a symptom of, that 'pallid lack of mood' – is also a kind of affect.

The question whether 'flat affect' might be identical with or a symptom of 'pallid lack of mood' affords an opportunity to relate Heidegger's discussion of affective states in *Nietzsche I* back to that in *Being and Time*. If 'flat affect' were identical with 'pallid lack of mood', then, apparently, affect would be identical to mood. If 'flat affect' were a symptom of 'pallid lack of mood', then, apparently, affect would relate to mood in something like the way that mood relates to affectedness, that is, as an indication of a more general structure. I have already suggested that affect might relate to passion in this sort of way, in positing that an affect might be the germ of a passion. A moment of anger may give birth to a persistent hatred. Moreover, the persistent hatred might manifest itself in future moments of anger.

It might be tempting to think that if affect is the more particular manifestation of the more general structure of passion, then affect should map on to mood and passion should map on to affectedness. However, the passion of *Nietzsche I* cannot be the affectedness of *Being and Time*. Passions are not ontological structures which we must discern hermeneutically from experienced phenomena; they are themselves phenomena that we experience. We do not only 'feel' affects like anger; we also 'feel' passions like love and hate. Indeed, Heidegger says that 'instead of "affect" and "passion" we also say "feeling", if not "sensation" [*Empfindung*]'.[56] There are quotation marks around the word 'feel' because the idea that happiness is a 'feeling', as that word is commonly understood, is just what we are trying to get away from. However, Heidegger suggests in *Nietzsche I* that we ought to understand the word 'feeling', *Gefühl*, in a different way: 'today', he writes,

> if we apply the term 'feeling' to a passion, it is understood as a kind of reduction. . . . Nevertheless, the simple fact that we refrain from calling

passions feelings does not prove that we possess a more highly developed concept of the essence of passion; it may only be a sign that we have employed too paltry a concept of the essence of feeling.[57]

What phenomena *might* the word 'feeling' help bring into view? Heidegger suggests the following:

[A] feeling is the way we find ourselves in relationship to beings, and thereby at the same time to ourselves. It is the way we find ourselves particularly attuned [*gestimmt*] to beings which we are not and to the being we ourselves are. In feeling, a state opens up, and stays open, in which we stand related to things, to ourselves, and to the people around us, always simultaneously.[58]

Thus we find something surprising here: it seems that Heidegger's analysis of *Gefühl* is identical to that of *Stimmung* in *Being and Time*, an impression which may be confirmed when Heidegger concludes that 'willing is feeling (state of attunement [*Gestimmtheit*])'.[59]

Now we may answer our question about the relation between affect and passion on one hand and mood on the other: affect and passion, as two kinds of what *Nietzsche I* calls feeling, are also two kinds of what *Being and Time* calls mood. What of deep happiness, then? Since I hope to show that it involves an attentiveness to being, it is tempting to say that deep happiness has the lucidity of a passion rather than the blindness of an affect. On the other hand, however, classifying it as a passion would raise one of the same problems as classifying it as a way of being affected. Passions *can* be felt, but they do not go away when they are not felt. We do not always feel our love for our loved ones, but we still love them when we do not feel it. If happiness were a passion, then we would be happy even when we did not feel happy. Thus deep happiness does not seem to be precisely either an affect or a passion, though we can say at least this much: happiness *involves* feelings, and we could not *be* happy if we did not *feel* happy. But this does not mean that happiness *is* a feeling.

What is Philosophy?: Stimmung vs Affekt or Gefühl

Near the beginning of *What is Philosophy?*, Heidegger says that inquiry into the nature of philosophy 'must . . . be of such a kind and direction that that of which philosophy treats concerns [*angeht*] us personally, affects [*berührt*[60]] us . . . in our very essence'.[61] Then he poses the question whether 'philosophy thereby becomes a matter of affection [*Affektion*], of affects [*Affekte*] and feelings [*Gefühle*]', noting that 'everyone considers the assertion correct that philosophy is a matter of reason', where reason is thought to be independent of, and indeed to require the absence of, affects. At this point Heidegger notes that reason cannot define philosophy if our conception of reason 'was first established only by philosophy and within the course of its history'.[62] This is Heidegger's bridge to an extended examination of philosophy's ancient Greek roots, which leads him to conclude that the basis of philosophy is the correspondence (*Entsprechung*) with being which is essential to human being. Having concluded this excursus, Heidegger returns to the question of the affective states and their relation to philosophy. He begins with a general discussion of mood which recalls that of *Being and Time*. Our correspondence with being, Heidegger says, is always attuned [*gestimmtes*]; it is in an attunement [*Gestimmtheit*]: 'as something attuned [*ge-stimmtes*] and tuned-in [*be-stimmtes*], correspondence essentially is in a mood [*Stimmung*]'.[63] Mood structures (*gefügt*) our attitude or comportment (*Verhalten*) towards being. Mood is not to be understood, Heidegger says, as the 'music of accidentally emerging feelings which only accompany the correspondence. If we characterize philosophy as tuned correspondence, then we by no means want to surrender thinking to the accidental changes and vacillations of feelings'.[64] Thus feelings are characterized in this text as, at most, epiphenomenal to our correspondence with being – feelings are precisely what both *Being and Time* and *What is Philosophy?* are concerned to show that mood is not. To emphasize this point we might note that 'feelings' here cannot be identified with what *Nietzsche I* calls 'affects', despite their apparent similarity. Feelings here are both impetuous and, we might say, blind, but they are not blind in the way that the affects of *Nietzsche I* are. An affect, there, is blind in the sense that it does not allow for self-conscious reflection on the way that it relates us to the world; a feeling, here, is blind in the sense that it does not relate us to the world at all. It is doubtful, however, that this represents Heidegger's own view on feelings – rather, it seems likely that he is contrasting his sense of mood with the *ordinary* view on feelings. However, in this text, he does *abandon* 'feelings' to the ordinary view, which he does not in the *Nietzsche* lectures.

Another aspect of the discussion of affective states in *What is Philosophy?* is Heidegger's proposal that each of philosophy's historical phases has a particular mood out of which the epoch of being it belongs to can be responded to appropriately. In *Being and Time*, Heidegger considers *Angst* to be the key way of being affected not only for the understanding of being

in our time, but for any possible understanding of being. In the 1929–
1930 lecture course published as *The Fundamental Concepts of Metaphysics*,
Heidegger identifies boredom (*Langeweile*) as the fundamental mood
(*Grundstimmung*) that shows up the temporal meaning of being in that particular, interwar time.[65] But the deepened understanding of the happening of being as *Ereignis* that Heidegger arrives at in the mid-1930s calls
for a reconception of the role that affective states play in our reception of
being. The affective states Heidegger privileges are now no longer ones
that afford a particular insight into temporality. When Heidegger has just
begun the thought of *Ereignis*, in the *Contributions*, he is most concerned
with 'startled dismay' as the fundamental mood that shows up the 'oblivion of being' that has prevailed throughout the metaphysical history of
the West. This 'startled dismay', Heidegger proposes, ought to replace the
'wonder' with which metaphysical philosophy began.[66]

The notion of the history of being adds another layer to Heidegger's view
of the role affective states play. In *What is Philosophy?*, recalling Socrates's
famous comment in the *Theaetetus*, Heidegger notes that for both Plato and
Aristotle, wonder or 'astonishment' (*Erstaunen*, θαυμάζειν) is the mood
(πάθος) proper to philosophy, the mood that both begins and sustains
it: it is philosophy's ἀρχή.[67] But philosophy, Heidegger proposes, does not
always have its ἀρχή in wonder. The mood of modern philosophy Heidegger
identifies as the Cartesian one of doubt.[68] Today, however, Heidegger
suggests, we cannot identify the predominant mood of philosophy – the
predominant mood in which we experience being and out of which our
correspondence to being is expressed. 'Presumably a fundamental mood
prevails', Heidegger says; 'it is, however, still hidden from us', as we encounter only a range of conflicting moods from which our correspondence with
being is expressed – doubt and dogmatism, fear and hope.[69] The mood
which Heidegger suggests may determine our correspondence with being
most 'often and widely' is the 'coldness' or 'prosaic sobriety [*prosaische
Nüchternheit*]' in which we correspond to being as something to be calcu-
lated and managed.[70]

Might deep happiness, then, be a fundamental mood for a new era of
philosophy, the successor to astonishment and doubt? No. Deep happiness
does not attune us to a particular *way* in which being happens to us. Rather,
it attunes us to the fact *that* being happens to us at all. It does not attune us
to one of the historical modes of being 'sent' to us or 'destined' for us in
Ereignis; it attunes us to *Ereignis*, the happening of being, itself.[71]

Chapter 1

Εὐδαιμονία and Happiness

This book's thesis about Heidegger and deep happiness is prefigured in important ways by ancient Greek thought concerning εὐδαιμονία. Εὐδαιμονία is the word normally translated as 'happiness'. This translation is notoriously problematic, since the Greeks, particularly Plato, Aristotle and the Stoics, often speak of εὐδαιμονία in ways that make it sound very different from what we normally think of as happiness. They tend to think of εὐδαιμονία as largely if not entirely an 'objective' state, while we tend to think of happiness as being more or less exclusively a 'subjective' one. As my notion of deep happiness is developed over the course of this book, it should become evident that there is a deeper kinship between εὐδαιμονία and happiness than is widely recognized, in their shared relation to fittingness. In any event, the history of thinking concerning something that might be called happiness begins with Greek thinking concerning εὐδαιμονία. The first two sections of this chapter will discuss some Greek thinking concerning εὐδαιμονία that reveals it to be very close to my sense of deep happiness. The third section will lay out the modern way of thinking about happiness, identifying Hobbes's role in shaping it, and will begin to indicate its inadequacy – especially where *deep* happiness is concerned.

Δαίμων and Εὐδαιμονία

As Marcus Aurelius points out, εὐδαιμονία literally means having a good δαίμων.[1] What does it mean to have a good δαίμων? What, in the first place, is a δαίμων? A δαίμων is, generally speaking, a divine being which is somehow less than a θεός, a god.[2] However, the word δαίμων is used in a variety of ways in ancient texts. It appears in a number of Plato's dialogues, and he uses it to refer to a number of different things. What unites them all is that the δαίμων is always characterized as something relating human beings to gods. In the *Symposium*, Diotima and Socrates decide that Ἔρως is a δαίμων, and not a god as Socrates had thought, because Ἔρως lacks things which are good and beautiful, while a god lacks no good and beautiful things. Not being a mortal, either, Ἔρως must be something in between, and to be something in between gods and mortals is to be a δαίμων.[3] In the *Timaeus*, Timaeus calls the soul a δαίμων: he says that the god 'has given to each of us, as his δαίμων, that kind of soul which is housed in the top of our body and which raises us – seeing that we are not an earthly but a heavenly plant up from earth towards our kindred in heaven'.[4] Moreover, he says that to properly care (θεραπεύειν) for the δαίμων makes one especially εὐδαίμων.[5] Aurelius identifies reason as a δαίμων, writing that it is a particle of Zeus, residing within oneself, which one needs to care for (again, θεραπεύειν); this care for the δαίμων, he says, is the task of philosophy.[6]

Of course, Socrates's remarks about his own δαίμων are well-known, particularly those in the *Apology* and the *Republic*, where he claims that his δαίμων has kept him from engaging in politics.[7] Socrates also refers to his δαίμων in the *Phaedrus*: after telling Phaedrus that he is going to go back to the city from the countryside where Phaedrus has taken him, Socrates announces that his δαίμων has prevented him from doing so until he has – as Fowler's translation has it – 'clear[ed] [his] conscience'.[8] The latter phrase translates the single word ἀφοσιώσωμαι, which Hackforth, for instance, renders as 'made atonement'.[9] The sense of the passage is not so much that the δαίμων calls on him to clear his conscience, but rather that the voice of the δαίμων *is* his conscience.[10] In both the *Apology* and the *Phaedrus*, Socrates refers to his δαίμων as a 'voice' which 'always holds me back from what I am thinking of doing, but never urges me forward'.[11] The voice does not tell Socrates anything in particular, but rather catches him up, gives him pause and makes him reconsider what he is going to do.

Thus his δαίμων acts in just the same way as, in *Being and Time*, Heidegger says conscience does. Heidegger writes: '*What* does conscience call to the one summoned? Strictly speaking – nothing . . . . "Nothing" is called *to* the self which is summoned, but it is *summoned* to itself, that is, to its ownmost potentiality-of-being'.[12] Conscience, in other words, is that by which one is called to one's freedom, founded on the self-transcending nature of human existence, and responsibility for one's finite existence. For now it will suffice to say that the δαίμων, understood as that which presents itself to us as the call of conscience, is that in human being which exceeds our facticity: it is that in us which, we might say, transcends the 'earthly', 'merely physical' aspect of our existence; it is that by which our existence is 'stretched' between earth and divine, facticity and transcendence (as Heidegger writes in the *Contributions*: '*Da-Sein* is the *between* between man . . . and gods'[13]). As Diotima tells Socrates, 'being midway between [gods and humans], [the δαίμων] makes each to supplement the other, so that the whole is combined in one'. Because our self-transcendence takes place through the δαίμων, and because self-transcendence is our distinctively human feature, the δαίμων is the aspect of human being that is most us, insofar as we are human.

To say that the δαίμων is that which is most us recalls a fragment of Heraclitus, which Heidegger discusses in his 'Letter on "humanism"': 'ἦθος ἀνθρώπῳ δαίμων', which is commonly translated as 'a person's character is his divinity'.[14] Heidegger charges that the translation of ἦθος by 'character' is tendentious, claiming that 'this translation thinks in a modern way, not a Greek one', and proposing that ἦθος rather 'means abode, dwelling place'.[15] Indeed, 'abode' and 'character' represent two of the three main clusters of accepted senses of ἦθος.[16] However, it is unnecessary to read 'character' and 'abode' as conflicting translations; rather, in light of the fact that ἦθος means 'abode' as well as 'character', we may understand 'character' in a richer manner, such that one's character is related to one's (manner of) dwelling, as indeed we see when Heidegger continues: 'the open region of his abode allows what pertains to the essence of the human being' – which, we might say, is the same thing as the character of the human being as human being – 'and what in thus arriving resides in nearness to him, to appear. The abode of the human being contains and preserves the advent of what belongs to the human being in his essence'.

Heidegger goes on to say that what belongs to the human essence 'is δαίμων, the god'. Of course, characterizing the δαίμων as a god seems inconsistent with the view I have been developing.[17] In his *Parmenides* lectures, Heidegger suggests a certain equivalence between θεοί and δαίμονεν on the basis of the similarity between, on one hand, θέα (goddess) and θεά (view), and on the other, δαίμως and δαίω (which Heidegger glosses as 'to present oneself in the sense of pointing and showing').[18] Thus, for Heidegger,

> θεοί, so-called 'gods', as the ones who look into the unconcealed and thereby give a sign, are θεάοντεν, are by essence δαίοντες-δαίμονες, the uncanny ones who present themselves in the ordinary. Both words, θεάοντες and δαίοντες, express the same thing, if thought of essentially.[19]

Notice, however, that the similarity Heidegger brings out between θεοί and δαίμονες does not make the latter more like what gods are conventionally conceived to be like; rather, it makes the θεοί more like δαίμονες on my account of the latter. This is a point to which I will return in Chapter 3, when I take up Heidegger's notion known as 'the fourfold'.

The relationship between δαίμων as I have interpreted that concept here and εὐδαιμονία appears strikingly, though implicitly, in Aristotle's *Nicomachean Ethics*. Aristotle says that the greatest human happiness comes from the activity of θεορία. As J. L. Ackrill has noted, it seems that θεορία cannot be, strictly speaking, distinctively human, because the god also engages in θεορία.[20] Moreover, since the god engages in nothing but θεορία, θεορία is more distinctive of the god than of human beings. In fact, Aristotle goes on to say that the life of θεορία 'will be higher than the human level: not in virtue of his humanity will a man achieve it, but in virtue of something within him' – that is, the 'intellect', νοῦς – 'that is divine', and he argues that the life of moral virtue is only secondary in εὐδαιμονία because 'the moral activities are purely human'.[21] Yet what is distinctively human, for Aristotle, is that human beings are not purely human: human beings transcend their own humanity, where the realm of humanity is conceived as being separate from the divine realm. What is distinctive of human existence, as opposed to the kind of existence shared by the 'lower animals', is precisely that it is *not* separate from the divine, but stretched between two realms. Thus, in Aristotle's apparently paradoxical conclusion, 'it may even be held that [the νοῦς] is what each [human being] is [εἶναι]'.[22] What is most fitting for human beings, then, is the activity in which we transcend our 'mere' humanity, that is, θεορία – and this, also, is the activity in which we fit together with divine things in our 'contemplation' of them.

Εὐδαιμονία and Fittingness in Plato's *Republic*

One of the main lines of thought running through Plato's *Republic* is that δικαιοσύνη – the virtue called 'justice' in English – is required for εὐδαιμονία: one must be just to be happy.[23] There is debate among commentators as to whether Plato means to suggest that δικαιοσύνη produces εὐδαιμονία, or that one is εὐδαίμων simply in virtue of being δίκαιος. I propose that his suggestion is that εὐδαιμονία and δικαιοσύνη are intimately related as two different kinds of fittingness.

At the end of Book I of the *Republic*, Socrates introduces the famous 'ἔργον (function) argument' – which Aristotle repeats in the first book of the *Nicomachean Ethics* – for the thesis that one must be just to be happy. The argument, which is deductive in form, is as follows. The ἔργον of the soul is to live. The virtue (ἀρετή) of a thing is that which enables it to carry out its function well. The virtue of the soul is δικαιοσύνη.[24] Therefore, to live well (εὖ ζῶν), one must be just. Furthermore, 'he who lives well is blessed and εὐδαίμων'; therefore, 'the just [person] is εὐδαίμων and the unjust miserable'.[25] Book I concludes, however, with Socrates pronouncing himself dissatisfied with this argument. It is indeed far too quick and easy – not without justification does Thrasymachus deride it as 'entertainment' (εἱστιάσθω). But what really dissatisfies Socrates is not the logic of the argument, but the fact that he had embarked upon it without first determining what justice is.

Though Socrates *says* at the end of Book I that he still does not know what the just is, the form of the definition of justice he will go on to formulate in Book IV – that is, that justice consists in 'doing one's own work' – is already present in the ἔργον argument. There, however, it is *happiness*, rather than justice, that consists in doing one's own work – in other words, living as is *fitting* for one as a human being. Of course, this is not presented as a definition of happiness, and it does not establish that happiness is identical to justice. However, the parallel between the definition of justice and the ἔργον argument for the happiness of the just life shows that, for Plato, the link between justice and happiness is not contingent. Justice does not merely *produce* happiness; happiness and justice are, rather, conceptually bound together by virtue of the fact that both consist in being as it is fitting for one to be.

Tempting though it is to dismiss the ἔργον argument and to suppose that the real arguments for the happiness of the just life are to be found later in the *Republic*, it is crucial to realize that, in fact, the ἔργον argument is not separable from Socrates's other arguments for the view that one must be just to be happy, or that it is 'advantageous' or 'pleasant' to be just. Socrates's problem with the ἔργον argument, as it stands at the end of Book I, is that it is not founded on a sufficiently developed account of the characteristically human virtue, that is, justice. But it is the main task of the rest of the *Republic* to develop just such an account. In other words, the ἔργον argument does not end at the closing of Book I; rather, the rest of the *Republic* is devoted to working out the terms of the argument.

Much of Book II is devoted to the development by Glaucon and Adeimantus of the common view that it is the unjust, and not the just, who are most happy – that, indeed, one will be happiest if one is unjust but thought to be just, while one will be unhappiest if one is just but thought to be unjust. Thus the common view assumes that happiness and unhappiness are not *intrinsically* related to justice and injustice, but rather are *consequences* of being thought to be just or unjust. It is Socrates's task, then, to show that justice is in that class of goods which are good (in the sense of being beneficial for the person who has them) intrinsically, and not just for their consequences. Socrates must do this in order to defend against the claim that justice is incompatible with happiness, as happiness is commonly understood, which is to say, as εὐδαιμονία was commonly understood among the Greeks, who ordinarily took material prosperity to be a central component of the εὐδαίμων life. The disjunction between Socrates's revisionary idea of εὐδαιμονία, in which it is analytically tied to δικαιοσύνη, and the one pressed by his interlocutors, in which εὐδαιμονία and δικαιοσύνη are at odds, comes up again and again in the *Republic*. We see this not only in Thrasymachus's scoffing in Book I, which forms the basis of the position pressed by Glaucon and Adeimantus in Book II, but also, for instance, in Glaucon's objection to the austerity of the state as Socrates begins to describe it: that state's material poverty makes it incompatible with the vulgar conception of εὐδαιμονία. This objection prompts Socrates to switch to the description of a 'fevered' city, which, Socrates says, has the benefit of allowing them to see how injustice arises in the city. And notice that what marks the 'fevered' city as unjust is that it does not fit inside its own borders – it must always be conquering new territory – as a result of the fact that its citizens' appetites are not made to fit within their own natural boundaries – they 'disregard the limit set by [their] necessary wants',[26] in the misguided belief that they will achieve εὐδαιμονία by doing so.

However, Socrates's idea of εὐδαιμονία, if it is indeed to be an idea that the word εὐδαιμονία is capable of invoking, must be distilled from the phenomena that people actually refer to as εὐδαιμονία. To philosophically deepen the ordinary conception of εὐδαιμονία, it must capture an important aspect of those phenomena that is usually obscured by less important or incidental aspects of them. Among those less important aspects is the association of the εὐδαίμων life with pleasure, ἡδονή, in general. People disregard the limits set by their necessary wants because they are pursuing pleasure, and as far as they are concerned εὐδαιμονία consists in a life of pleasure.

If we have only a passing familiarity with Plato, then we might expect Plato to deny that the pursuit of pleasure has anything to do with εὐδαιμονία, but in fact this is not the case. Plato's idea of εὐδαιμονία denies the identification of εὐδαιμονία with ἡδονή, but it would be implausible as an idea of εὐδαιμονία – and certainly it would be implausible for us as an idea of happiness – if it failed to acknowledge some relationship between εὐδαιμονία and ἡδονή. In fact, Plato's view on the relationship between ἡδονή and εὐδαιμονία will be significant for my purposes, for this reason: the deep happiness I am concerned with involves what we might call pleasure, in a certain sense – the exemplary situations of which I will provide phenomenological sketches can all be described as profoundly pleasurable, though not in a way usually associated with 'hedonism'. As we will see, Plato provides us with a model of a conception of happiness in which pleasure plays an essential role, but which is not 'hedonist' in the usual modern sense of that word.

In Book IX of the *Republic*, Socrates offers three arguments for the thesis that being just is always preferable to being unjust. The first argument is that tyrants are the unhappiest of people because their souls are disordered – they are enslaved by their appetites. The latter two arguments purport to show that the pleasures of just people – that is, particularly, philosophers – are superior to the pleasures of the unjust. It is controversial among Plato scholars whether these arguments commit Plato to a version of hedonism – if not to the equation of εὐδαιμονία with ἡδονή, then at least to the position that ἡδονή contributes to εὐδαιμονία, and may even be necessary for it. The controversy hinges on the question whether the two arguments for the pleasantness of the just life are supposed to be arguments for the just life's happiness – that is, whether the just life is happy (at least in part) *because* it is pleasant – or whether they are supposed to show that the just life is *preferable* to the unjust life because it is more pleasant *in addition to* being happier. James Butler has recently argued – convincingly, in my view – that the arguments for the pleasantness of the just life are also arguments for its happiness. This being the case, according to Butler, Plato endorses some kind of hedonism, although this hedonism 'must differ from what might be called the "somatic hedonism" rejected [in other dialogues]'.[27] Indeed, the resistance to admitting pleasure as any part of Plato's conception of happiness could only be due to the identification of hedonism with 'somatic hedonism'. No doubt the word 'pleasure' usually brings to mind sensual pleasures first and foremost. But in the language of Plato ἡδονή serves to name both sensual pleasures and intellectual ones.

The first argument for the superiority of philosophical pleasures is that philosophers necessarily have experienced the pleasures of material goods and of honour as well as those of contemplation, and prefer the latter.[28] This argument is echoed by Mill: he follows his famous declaration that it is 'better to be a human being dissatisfied than a pig satisfied; better to be Socrates dissatisfied than a fool satisfied' with the comment that 'if the fool, or the pig, is of a different opinion, it is because they only know their own side of the question'.[29] For Mill, the supposed fact that the higher pleasures are preferred to lower ones by those who have experienced both is the sole basis on which the distinction between higher and lower pleasures can be supported. However, this argument does not tell us *why* the higher pleasure, or the life of the philosopher, is preferred; though Mill says that there is a qualitative difference between higher and lower pleasures, he does not attempt to explain what the qualitative difference is.[30]

Plato, on the other hand, provides us with a further argument which does pertain to the quality of philosophical pleasure: an object of the kind in which philosophical pleasure is taken 'more truly *is*' than the objects of other kinds of pleasure.[31] It has already been determined, in Book V, that knowledge concerns that which most fully is, whereas opinion concerns that which is 'between' that which is and that which is not.[32] Thus the philosopher, seeking knowledge, seeks that which more truly is than the objects of opinion.

But what does it mean to 'more truly be'? What makes it more truly the case that it is is that it is 'ever like itself and immortal', while what less truly is is 'mortal and never the same'.[33] In other words, it more truly is insofar as it more fully instantiates that 'constant presence' which, as Heidegger tells us, Western metaphysics has always identified with being: that which most truly is remains as it is forever. Thus one gets more and better pleasure from the philosophical contemplation of what most truly is than one gets from other sources, not only because the objects of philosophical pleasure last longer – indeed, they are eternal – but also because 'that which is more really filled with real things would more really and truly cause us to enjoy a true pleasure'.[34] The philosophical pleasures are both 'stable' and 'pure'.[35]

There are two important ideas here for my purposes. First, for Plato, to take pleasure in something means to appropriate its being. (Of course, this means something very different on Plato's terms than on Heidegger's, since for Plato the being of a being is itself a being, and for Plato, unlike Heidegger, the appropriation is not mutual.) Second, pleasure, like happiness and justice, is a kind of fittingness. Pleasure, according to Plato, consists in the fulfillment of a fitting desire; 'to be filled with what befits nature [φύσει προσηκόντων] is pleasure'.[36] It is the nature of the appetitive part of the soul to want material things, and so the enjoyment of material things is fitting for it. The spirited part of the soul naturally wants honour and victory, and so it is fitting for it to gain these things. The rational part of the soul naturally wants to know the forms of things, and so it is fitting for it to contemplate the forms.

Since ἡδονή is a kind of fittingness, there is a close conceptual connection between it and εὐδαιμονία, just as there is between δικαιοσύνη and εὐδαιμονία. But just as εὐδαιμονία is not equivalent to δικαιοσύνη, neither is ἡδονή equivalent to εὐδαιμονία. For one thing, there are more and less fitting kinds of ἡδονή, and it is up to the rational part of the soul to discern between them and to aid the other two parts in obtaining the most fitting ones. Socrates says that if the appetitive and spirited parts 'take only those pleasures which reason approves', then they 'will, since they follow truth, enjoy the truest pleasures, so far as that is possible for them, and also the pleasures that are proper to them and their own'.[37] When the rational part is allowed to guide the others in this way, 'the entire soul . . . is not filled with inner dissension, [and] the result for each part is that it in all other respects keeps to its own task and is just, and likewise that each enjoys its own proper pleasures'.[38]

This passage should make clear the intimate relation that Plato holds to exist between pleasure and happiness. We already know that the necessary and sufficient condition of εὐδαιμονία is δικαιοσύνη; now Socrates tells us that δικαιοσύνη is at least the necessary condition for each part of the soul to gain for itself the best and most fitting ἡδονή. Thus the difference between ἡδονή and εὐδαιμονία on the scheme that emerges from the *Republic* is that a ἡδονή is specific to a particular part of the soul, while εὐδαιμονία can only be predicated of the person as a whole. Recall Socrates's remark that he is not concerned about the happiness of this or that individual, but that of the city as a whole.[39] Readings of the *Republic* as a work of 'political philosophy' regard this comment as merely an expression of Plato's supposed anti-individualism or 'communism'. But we should remember that the motive for the description of the city, and of the way that justice and injustice arise in it, is to be able to see, in macrocosm, how justice and injustice arise in the individual soul. Thus when Socrates says that he is concerned with the happiness of the entire city, the significance of his remark is that he is concerned with the happiness of the entire soul, not of this or that part of it. And indeed this or that part of the soul could not be said to be εὐδαίμων, because εὐδαιμονία consists in the soul as a whole carrying out its proper function well.

We may now summarize the relationship between εὐδαιμονία, δικαιοσύνη and ἡδονή as follows: εὐδαιμονία consists in the soul as a whole being as is fitting for it, which means carrying out its ἔργον in accordance with its particular ἀρετή, namely δικαιοσύνη; δικαιοσύνη consists in each part of the soul doing what is fitting for it, which means carrying out its own task toward the fulfilment of the whole soul's ἔργον and not interfering with the other parts as they carry out their tasks; and ἡδονή results from the success of a particular part of the soul in carrying out its task and appropriating the being of an object of the sort that is fitting for it.

Modern Happiness

We have seen how, for the ancient Greeks, εὐδαιμονία is intimately tied to two kinds of fitting: εὐδαιμονία can be seen to consist in being as is fitting for one, and also to consist in a fitting relation between the human and the divine. This seems very distant from the modern conception of happiness. In this section, I will examine the modern conception and its roots in Hobbes, beginning to suggest how it is deficient, and that we ought to retrieve something of the sense the Greeks had of εὐδαιμονία. The case that it is appropriate to identify this sense with the word 'happiness' will be made in the next chapter, when I examine the etymological roots of 'happiness'.

Robert Nozick distinguishes between three kinds of happiness: 'being happy that something or other is the case'; 'feeling that your life is good now'; and 'being satisfied with your life as a whole'.[40] For all three kinds, Nozick holds happiness to be a 'feeling' or an 'emotion', though he also suggests that happiness can be the 'mood' consisting in 'the proneness or tendency' to have the emotion of happiness.[41] L. W. Sumner, meanwhile, identifies four different 'dimensions' of happiness relevant to philosophical inquiry into happiness: 'being happy with or about something'; 'feeling happy'; 'having a happy disposition'; and 'being happy' (in general) or 'having a happy life'.[42] But the sense of 'happiness' in all these dimensions, according to Sumner, must accord with what he claims is the one thing about which 'modern theories of happiness' agree, namely, 'that happiness is subjective'.[43]

Sumner's claim, which is indeed reflected by the great majority of contemporary philosophical work on happiness, is, in essence, that modern happiness is 'hedonist' and not 'eudaimonist': happiness consists in subjective pleasurable feelings, not in objective good ways of being. This conception of happiness is most closely associated with the utilitarians beginning with Bentham, but its dominance preceded them. Already in Locke, hedonism is taken for granted, both as a theory of happiness and as a theory of the foundations of ethics. In the *Essay Concerning Human Understanding*, Locke writes:

> [W]hat has an aptness to produce pleasure in us is that we call good, and what is apt to produce pain in us we call evil; for no other reason but for its aptness to produce pleasure and pain in us, wherein consists our happiness and misery.[44]

Wladyslaw Tatarkiewicz, whose *Analysis of Happiness* is the last century's most comprehensive philosophical treatment of happiness, notes that in the eighteenth century, 'the concept [of happiness] which established itself . . . had no room for anything but pleasures', not only among anglophone philosophers but across Europe.[45]

Hobbes is probably the philosopher who, more than any other, laid the groundwork for the dominance of the hedonistic view of happiness. In *Leviathan*, Hobbes writes that 'felicity' consists in '*continuall successe* in obtaining those things which a man from time to time desireth, that is to say, continuall prospering'.[46] Hobbes rejects eudaimonism with the following declaration, aimed at the Aristotelianism of the scholastics: 'the Felicity of this life, consisteth not in the repose of a mind satisfied. For there is no such *Finis ultimus*, (utmost ayme,) nor *Summum Bonum* (greatest Good,) as is spoken of in the Books of the old Morall Philosophers.'[47]

Hobbes rejects eudaimonism because his radical empiricism compels him to reject the metaphysics on which it rests. For Hobbes, the only possible objects of our knowledge are the 'bodies' 'which presseth the organ proper to each sense',[48] and so we are constrained to believe in the existence of nothing but bodies in motion. In this scheme there is no room for a τέλος of human beings. Nor is there any room for anything like a δαίμων which, as we have seen, is of the essence of εὐδαιμονία. After Hobbes, secular philosophers no longer conceive of human beings, as the ancients did, as being 'stretched' between the earthly and the divine; the earthly is all that there is. We relate to the world as bodies in motion among other bodies in motion; in the perpetual turmoil of being, pleasure is fleeting and hard to come by, while pains always threaten, and so we can never rest content with present pleasures: 'felicity is a continuall progresse of the desire, from one object to another; the attaining of the former, being still but the way to the later'.[49]

Today the subjectivist, hedonistic view descended from Hobbes is so dominant that some refuse to recognize the debate between objectivist and subjectivist views of happiness as being debates about *happiness* at all, insisting that they must rather be about *the good life* or *well-being.*[50] Though I aim to transcend the distinction between subjectivist and objectivist views of happiness, it will be helpful to try to get clear about the question of the objectivity of happiness. The question is more complicated than it may appear, and once pressed it becomes very complicated indeed. I will point out two different general senses the question may have, and just a couple of the complications they engender.

First, the question may be (and is most usually) about whether happiness consists in, on one hand, a *feeling* or *psychological state* or, on the other hand, some set of conditions of one's life. If the question is decided in favour of the former, then happiness is said to be subjective. Second, the question may be about whether or not our judgements concerning our own happiness are fallible. That is, the question may be about whether or not it is possible for people to *be* happy without being *inclined to judge* themselves happy, and vice versa. Happiness may be held to be objective in this sense even though it is subjective in the first sense. (If happiness is held to be objective in the first sense, it will usually be held to be objective in the second sense as well, since the objective situation in which happiness consists will generally be thought to be objectively recognizable.) Assuming that happiness consists in a psychological state, there can still be disagreement over whether some *particular* psychological state objectively qualifies as happiness, or whether it is up to individuals to decide what psychological state(s) they count as happiness. The usual assumption that happy psychological states are *pleasurable* cannot accommodate, for instance, the Stoic thesis that the psychological state of ἀπάθεια is the key to εὐδαιμονία; these are two conflicting objectivist views as to the quality of the psychological state happiness consists in. The question in the second sense can, in turn, be either epistemologically or ontologically oriented: one's judgements about one's happiness may be infallible either because one has a unique epistemic access to one's own psychological states – that is, only I am in a position to know how I feel, and even though I may be wrong, you cannot overrule my judgement on the basis of objective (e.g. behavioural) evidence – or because judging oneself happy is all there is to *being* happy.

The debate concerning whether the ancient Greeks' εὐδαιμονία is the same thing as our 'happiness' concerns the question in its first sense. Aristotle (whose doctrine is usually the focus of the debate) holds that εὐδαιμονία consists primarily in a certain objective state – namely, a life of virtuous activity – while in ordinary contemporary usage the term 'happiness' refers primarily to psychological states. Richard Kraut attempts to bridge the gap between Aristotle's εὐδαιμονία and our 'happiness' by arguing that 'a *eudaimon* individual, as Aristotle conceives him, is in the very same psychological state as a person who is living happily' in the ordinary contemporary sense of the latter term.[51] L. W. Sumner responds that this is insufficient, because Aristotle's account, holding as it does that εὐδαιμονία requires the exercise of virtue, still conflicts with our intuition – which Sumner claims is part of the 'core' of our concept of happiness – that vicious people can experience the psychological state we ordinarily identify with happiness.[52] In other words, on Sumner's view, the conditions which for Aristotle constitute εὐδαιμονία may be *sufficient* for happiness in our sense, but they are not *necessary*.

As evidence that Aristotle's objectivist εὐδαιμονία is not equivalent to our 'happiness', Sumner points to the fact that recent social scientific research on happiness generally assumes that happiness is something subjective like 'perceived well-being' or 'assessed quality of life'.[53] As Sumner points out, such research has a prescriptive effect on our conception of happiness: it 'has not only taken over an antecedent subjective conception of happiness – it has also consolidated and entrenched it. In this way it has contributed to making an objective conception unintelligible to us'.[54] Thus Sumner acknowledges that the term 'happiness' used to be more flexible, that its meaning used to be richer, than it ordinarily is now. For Sumner, this loss of meaning is irreversible, at least by philosophical means (i.e. we might say, by 'artificial' means, as opposed to the 'organic' means by which the meaning of a word changes without anyone intending to change it), because – for him, as for practically all contemporary philosophers dealing with happiness – philosophy can only appeal to ordinary usage. According to Sumner, 'a basic requirement of adequacy for any theory about the nature of happiness' is that 'it must fit reasonably well with our preanalytic convictions', and that 'we manifest these convictions whenever we judge that our lives, or the lives of others, are happy or unhappy'.[55] In Sumner's view, our preanalytic convictions about what happiness is have a more or less discernable 'core' and 'periphery', where 'one sign . . . that we have moved from core to periphery is that our responses become tentative or divided'.[56] Theories of happiness may be 'revisionary' at the periphery of our conception of happiness, but not at the core; putative theories of happiness that attempt to revise the core are not theories of happiness at all.

If philosophers are going to have anything meaningful to say to people about happiness, and particularly if philosophers are going to be able to deepen people's understanding of happiness, we are going to have to do better than to repeat back to them what they already say – or what we, perhaps idiosyncratically, think they say. Of course, this does not mean that we can depart altogether from ordinary usage. If the expansion of the sense of 'happiness' that I am attempting here did not meet up with ordinary contemporary usage in any significant way, then there would be no common ground on which a fusion of horizons could take place and people could be convinced that our usual sense of happiness is impoverished. This point is similar to Sumner's argument that a theory of happiness can be revisionary at the periphery but not at the core of the ordinary concept. But I differ from Sumner in what I take to be the 'core'. For an analytic philosopher like Sumner, the core is what we see most often reflected in the most frequent uses of the word. The core is in plain view; it is precisely whatever is most plainly in view. But for me, the 'core' is not necessarily in plain view, but may rather require some work to uncover.

Chapter 2

The Happening of Being

Turning from Temporality to *Ereignis*

The common notion that Heidegger's thinking underwent a 'turn', beginning after the publication of *Being and Time* and ending more or less a decade later, risks conflating two different things.[1] The first is the turning – *die Kehre* – that Heidegger considered all along to be part of the *matter* of the project of *Being and Time* itself; the second is the 'shift in thinking' – *die Wendung in Denken* – that led Heidegger to modify if not abandon that project.[2] The turning that was supposed to be part of the matter of *Being and Time* was the turning, the reversibility, the reciprocity, between *Da-Sein's* temporal reception of being and the temporality of being itself. The shift occurred when Heidegger gave up his plan to think through that turning in the terms of *Being and Time*.[3]

It is indeed important to notice that when Heidegger himself speaks of '*die Kehre*' he is never talking about the shift in his own thinking. But on the other hand, the shift in his thinking happens to occur when he takes up '*die Kehre*' – when he turns to 'the turning'. Commentators have proposed some very complex theoretical and political answers to the question why Heidegger did not or could not carry out the description of the turning as originally planned.[4] I propose that the most illuminating answer is much simpler than we may suspect: Heidegger did not produce the projected description of the turning because he had come to realize that the kind of description he had had in mind would not turn out to be an adequate description of being.

Heidegger's enduring question is this: how can we adequately *describe* being? His essential insight, which forms the basis for his attempts to answer his enduring question, is that being *happens*. As Heidegger reminds us in various places, the word 'being', *Sein*, is a verb, indicating that it names, most properly, not a substance or a thing, nor a quality of things, but 'something' that things *do*. This is why, in the beginning of his career,

he considers *time* the key to the description of being. It is also what motiv-
ates his interpretation of Nietzsche's idea of eternal recurrence.[5] In that
interpretation, the underlying ontological significance of the doctrine of
eternal recurrence points towards his own doctrine of being and time.
That underlying ontological significance is that being is not *static.* To
oppose being and becoming, as the Platonic metaphysical tradition has
always done, obscures what it means to be. And yet Heidegger comes to
suggest that his own doctrine of *Being and Time* is part and parcel of the
metaphysical tradition he wants to overcome. Heidegger says in the 'Letter
on "humanism"' that he 'held back' the section of *Being and Time* that was
to work out the turning because it 'did not succeed with the help of the
language of metaphysics'.[6]

The reference to *language* is perplexing. Heidegger does, in his later
work, make claims about Western languages being inherently metaphysical. But is it merely a matter of terminology? Is only a new set of terms
required to think through the turning? What is at stake is an adequate
description of being. In order to understand what is at stake, then, we need to
understand what a description is, and what it means for a description to be
adequate. A description is not a statement of fact which is either accurate
or not. 'The cat is on the mat' is true if the cat is on the mat, but whether
'the cat is on the mat' is an adequate description of the situation is a more
difficult question. A description can be inadequate without being false,
without manifesting in words something substantially other than what is
actually the situation. A description of a situation is adequate if it makes us
aware of that which is important about the situation, but of which we have
not become aware on our own. So, in order to know whether a description
is adequate, we need to know not only whether it succeeds in making its
audience aware of what it is intended to, but also whether what it intends to
describe is actually what is most important. Thus whether the description
of being projected for the unpublished portion of *Being and Time* would be
adequate depends, first, on whether what it would bring into words is what
is most important about being, and, second, on whether it would actually
be capable of leading its audience to the intended awareness of being.

In what way, then, might *Being and Time*'s projected description of being
be inadequate? Heidegger says in the 'Letter' that the unpublished portion
of *Being and Time* 'was held back because thinking failed in the adequate
saying of [the] turning'.[7] We may get the idea from this statement that
Heidegger was unable to put into words the mirror image of *Da-Sein*'s temporality, namely the temporality of being itself, that was supposed to be
the subject of the next division of *Being and Time.* I think, however, that it

may be quite simple to put that mirror image into words. In the following example I will attempt to indicate how it might be done.

A glass is falling. I can describe the temporal structure of the event either in terms of my experience or in terms of the being of the glass. In terms of my experience, I understand the situation of the glass in mid-air only because my experience encompasses both the past and the future of the glass. On one hand, I am aware of it as having been on the table where it held my drink (and before that as having been given to me by someone at a certain time and place, giving it further dimensions of significance) and as having fallen off the table. On the other hand, I anticipate its hitting the ground and shattering, my having to clean it up, my having to beware of stepping on glass splinters that I don't see, my having one less glass and possibly needing to replace it. My understanding converges on the present from the past and the future. Similarly it converges on the future from the past and present – I expect the glass to hit the ground because I am aware of its being in mid-air and its having fallen off the table – and on the past from the present and the future – I understand that the glass has fallen off the table because I am aware of its being in mid-air and I expect that it will proceed downwards and shatter. Heidegger refers to the dimensions of *Da-Sein*'s temporality as *ecstases* because we are not temporally located only in the present, but also 'outside ourselves' in the past and future. As Heidegger puts it in *The Basic Concepts of Phenomenology*, our existence is 'stretched' between past, present and future.[8]

Conversely, in terms of the being of the glass, the glass *is* in mid-air, falling, because it *has* fallen off the table and because it *will* proceed to the floor. The glass cannot *be* as it *is* apart from its *having been* as it *was* and its *going to be* the way it *will be*. The past and the future of the glass are constituents of its present – the being of the glass is also a 'stretched' temporal happening. The falling glass does not simply move from one atom of time, one now, to the next. It has its past as what brought it where it is in the present, and it has its future as the potentialities that are open to it (just as its past has its present as its outcome, and its future has its present as the determinant of its potentialities). Maybe I could reach out and grab the glass, in which case this possibility, as well as the possibility of the glass hitting the floor and shattering, goes into the determination of both my experience of the falling glass and the being-falling-of-the-glass itself. The glass in mid-air *is* the potential for shattering glass; it *is* the potential for cleaning up broken glass, cut feet, buying a new glass and so on.

Thus the temporality of human existence and the temporality of being mirror each other. This mirroring *is* the *Kehre* that Heidegger planned to describe in *Being and Time*; the turning consists in the reversibility of our experience of being and being itself.

If it is as simple as that, however, why does Heidegger say that 'thinking failed in the adequate saying of the turning?' For a clue we might look at the 1949 lecture 'The turning'. On a cursory reading, the turning named in that lecture's title may seem to have little to do with the project of *Being and Time*. The theme of the lecture is 'the turning of the danger' of the technological epoch; we may get the idea that the turning is only a turning *out* of that epoch (and certainly Heidegger does speak of a turning in that sense). But Heidegger says that the turning 'comes to pass [*ereignet*] *in* the danger'; 'in this turning, the clearing belonging to the essence of being suddenly clears itself and lights up'.[9] Referring to the title of the lecture series which 'The turning' concludes, Heidegger says: '*Insight into that which is* – this designation now names the disclosing that brings into its own that is the *Ereignis* of the turning within being.'[10]

'*Ereignis*', which becomes the most important word for Heidegger's thinking from the mid-1930s onwards, names what takes place in the turning – it is the *event*, the *happening*, of the turning. Indeed, '*Ereignis*', in ordinary German, means 'event'. But resonating in it is the root '*eigen*', meaning 'own', which Heidegger often emphasizes by separating the prefix *Er-* from it with a hyphen. In accord with this emphasis, recent translations (notably Emad and Maly's translation of the *Contributions to Philosophy*) have rendered *Ereignis* as 'enowning', which captures the literal meaning of the prefix and root but lets escape the word's sense in ordinary German (as well as its ordinariness in German). Stambaugh attempts to capture both aspects with the phrase 'event of appropriation'; typically, it has been rendered simply as 'appropriation'.

Thomas Sheehan has issued an important challenge to all these renderings. The challenge is this: Sheehan argues that in one of Heidegger's unpublished works of the 1930s, Heidegger shows that it is inappropriate to translate *Ereignis* with the English 'appropriation' because 'the original etymon of *Ereignis* is not *eigen* . . . but rather *eräugen/ereugen*', the roots of which are shared with the contemporary German word *Auge* (eye) and have to do with seeing. Only by accident did the diphthong *äu/eu* 'devolve' into 'ei', and so the apparent *eigen* in *Ereignis* is merely homonymous with the *eigen* meaning 'own'.[11] Sheehan concludes that this 'makes it clear . . . that what Heidegger meant by *Ereignis* is not primarily "appropriation" or "enowning"'.

Clearly, however, Heidegger does not regard the apparent *eigen* in *Ereignis* as a mere accident. A more straightforward sense of 'appropriation' in

Ereignis is central, if not primary, in Heidegger's use of it, as is evident in passages which, in discussing *Ereignis*, invoke other words with the root *eigen*. A striking example occurs in the 1957 lecture 'The principle of identity':

> The *belonging* together [*Zusammen*gehören] of man and being in the manner of mutual challenge drives home to us with startling force that and how man is delivered over to the ownership [*vereignet*] of being and being is appropriate to [*zugeeignet*] the essence of man. Within the framework there prevails a strange ownership [*Vereignen*] and a strange appropriation [*Zueignen*]. We must experience simply this owning in which man and being are delivered over [*ge-eignet*] to each other, that is, we must enter into what we call the *Ereignis*.[12]

Immediately following this in the German original is a passage which, as Sheehan notes,[13] is missing from Stambaugh's translation, wherein Heidegger again points out that *äugen* is the original root of *Ereignis*. But the sentence in question, read in full, runs counter to Sheehan's argument. It is as follows: '*Er-eignen heißt ursprünglich: er-äugen, d.h. er-blicken, im Blicken zu sich rufen, an-eignen.*'[14] *Aneignen* is the ordinary German word meaning to appropriate; the sentence can be translated: '*Er-eignen* originally means: to take in with the eyes, to catch sight of, in the glance towards what calls – to a(p)-propriate.' In other words, the appropriation of being consists in our catching sight of what calls to be seen; we appropriate being (i.e. as we will see below, we enter into a mutual appropriation with being) when we catch sight of it. Thus, for Heidegger, an awareness of the etymological link of *Ereignis* with *äugen* should not restrict the sense of the word *Ereignis* by suggesting that we should not hear in it the *eigen* which we do hear, and which evidently speaks in Heidegger's use of it. Rather, the etymology should enrich our understanding of our mutual appropriation with being. It should remind us of a truth our forgetting of which is part and parcel of our forgetting of being: that seeing is, or can be, a kind of appropriation, namely, an appropriation, a taking-into-ownership (enowning), of being.[15]

We should not hear in 'appropriation' the usual connotation of taking ownership *away* from another; rather we might think of it in the sense that one may be said to appropriate another's love: in appropriating another's love for me I make it my own without removing it from the other; indeed, removed from the other it could no longer exist. Moreover, in genuine love there must be a similar appropriation of me by the other, or else the love cannot be love *for me*. In a similar way, *Ereignis* is a mutual appropriation: we appropriate being in our experience of it, and – which is the same thing – being appropriates us in its happening to us. As Heidegger puts it in 'The principle of identity', in *Ereignis*, 'man is delivered over to the ownership [*vereignet*] of being and being is appropriate[d] [*zugeeignet*] to the essence of man.'[16] Thus in the formulation 'being happens to us', we need to pay attention to the 'to', reading it in the sense of 'towards': things *are* 'towards' us, in our direction, so to speak; for the happening of their being to be completed, their being must be received, taken in, appropriated by us. Being comes into its own; it arrives at what is proper to itself, by appropriating our capacity to experience being so that the happening of being may be fulfilled. At the same time we come into our own, arriving at what is proper to us as human beings, by appropriating the happening of being in our experience of it so that our capacity for receiving the happening of being may be fulfilled.

In 'The turning', Heidegger describes this mutual appropriation of being and human being using the words *einblicken* and *einblitzen*, 'insight' and 'in-flashing': the turning, the reversibility between our experience and being, consists in the fact that our 'insight' into that which is is the same as the 'in-flashing' of the being of what is into us.[17] This sense of the turning within *Ereignis* can be seen in the following passage in the 1957 lecture 'The principle of identity': 'The *Ereignis* as *Er-eignis* is that realm [*Bereich*], swinging [*schwingende*] within itself, through which man and being reach [*erreichen*] each other in their essences, achieving their essences by losing those determinations [*Bestimmungen*] with which metaphysics has endowed them.'[18] *Er-eignis* 'swings' from one to the other in their 'reaching', their in-flashing and insight, towards each other.

In 1962, 35 years after the publication of *Being and Time*, Heidegger gave a lecture under the title 'Time and being' – the title of the unpublished section of *Being and Time* in which the turning was to be worked out. In that lecture, Heidegger first of all recapitulates *Being and Time*'s account of temporality, saying that 'future, past and present are before us "at the same time"', that 'they belong together in the way they offer themselves to one another', that 'the unity of time's three dimensions consists in the interplay of each toward each' – and that 'time-space' – that is, the 'four-dimensional space' of past, present, future, and the interplay between them – 'is the name for the openness which opens up in the mutual self-extending of futural approach, past and present'.[19] Thus, says Heidegger, 'true time appears as the "It" of which we speak when we say: "It gives being" [*Es gibt Sein*].'[20] (I will discuss the formulation '*Es gibt Sein*' in Chapter 3. For now it will suffice to note that *Es gibt* has the sense of the English 'there is', but is literally translated 'it gives'.)

On a *Being and Time*-like account, 'true', four-dimensional time allows for the happening of being and – which is the same thing – of that being's givenness to us. However, Heidegger continues, this cannot be the final answer to the question of being, because 'time itself remains the gift of an "It gives"'. *This* is the point on which the attempt to work through the turning on the terms of *Being and Time* founders – it is the point at which the description of being as temporal happening gives way to the description of being as happening-to-us. If time allows for the happening of being, what allows for the happening of time? Obviously time does not happen *temporally*, but nonetheless it happens – it happens in the sense that it comes to presence for us, a coming-to-presence which, for instance, allows us to describe it as four-dimensional. This happening in the sense of coming-to-presence is thus prior to temporal happening – and the happening of coming-to-presence, which is the same as happening-to-us, is *Ereignis*: 'What determines both, time and being' – here being is understood in the sense of the history of being – 'in their own, that is, in their belonging together, we shall call: *Ereignis*'.[21]

We can now conclude that when Heidegger says that 'thinking failed in the adequate saying of the turning and did not succeed with the help of the language of metaphysics', he does not mean only that a new language, a new set of terms, is needed. The very conception of the happening of being in *Being and Time* is metaphysical. For Heidegger, metaphysics characteristically seeks a ground for the being of beings – a ground that is itself a being. *Being and Time* conceives of *time* as such a being. This alone does not show that the description of being in the terms of *Being and Time* is inadequate; it is, rather, a theoretical way to account for the inadequacy. What *shows* the inadequacy is that such a description does not capture what is most important: that being happens to us.

Language, 'The Other Language' and Etymology

One might expect that Heidegger's announcement in the 'Letter' of the failure of the language of metaphysics would herald a present move into a different language, yet the editors of the *Gesamtausgabe* edition of *Wegmarken* supply a note (reproduced in the English translation) that Heidegger made on the first page of his copy of the text, stating that 'the letter continues to speak in the language of metaphysics, and does so knowingly. The other language remains in the background'.[22] What are we to make of this remark? As I have suggested, what Heidegger wants to describe about being is different after the 'turn' – his concern is still the question of being, but the question of being is now understood differently. To account for this difference, he begins, in the *Contributions*, to use the archaic spelling *Seyn* to 'indicate that being [*Seyn*] . . . is no longer thought metaphysically'.²³ From this point onwards, Heidegger is acutely aware that the very word *Sein*, 'being', as he would put it in 'A dialogue on language', 'belongs . . . to the patrimony of the language of metaphysics'.²⁴ Attempts to communicate the results of Heideggerian investigations into being are hindered, perhaps often fatally, from the outset by the fact that the word 'being' speaks metaphysically – we *hear* it metaphysically; what it *says* to us, by default, is either the objective actuality of things or their putative ground and source. It is one thing for Heidegger to tell us that there is a deeper sense of *Sein* than this, and even for us to take his word for it; it is quite another for us to actually *hear* this deeper sense in the word, which is to say, for being in that deeper sense to manifest itself to us through the word.

The spelling *Seyn* is used to indicate that we must try to hear this deeper sense of being. Yet Heidegger hardly ever uses the spelling *Seyn* in any of the works published in his lifetime. The only time he does, to my knowledge, is in a paragraph inserted into the concluding 'Note' in the second (1949) edition of 'The essence of truth'²⁵ – an exceptional exception which at least does not seem to count much against the rule that Heidegger does not write *Seyn* to his contemporary audiences. The same can be said of another device that Heidegger uses in part to indicate that *Sein* must be heard in a deeper sense, namely, making a cross through the word *Sein*. Despite its notoriety, this device is to be found only in one piece published by Heidegger, namely his open letter to Ernst Jünger titled 'On the question of being'.

For the general philosophical public, Heidegger writes *Sein* throughout his career – though, as we discover when we compare, for instance, the published text of *Einführung in die Metaphysik* with the manuscript pages appended to the *Gesamtausgabe* version, or the version of the lecture '*Die kehre*' published in the *Gesamtausgabe* with the one published in Heidegger's lifetime, Heidegger sometimes writes *Seyn* in his manuscript where *Sein* appears in the official publication.²⁶ The fact that Heidegger says *Sein* to others where he says *Seyn* to himself goes to show that his remarks about 'the language of metaphysics' (and the inherently metaphysical nature of Western languages²⁷) should not be taken to mean that what he wants to say requires another language – indeed, his own 'other language' – in order to be said at all. As we are about to see, this could not be the case, given Heidegger's view of language. Still, what Heidegger wants to say can be said more evocatively in that 'other language', as long as that 'other language' says anything to us at all, which, unless we are prepared to hear it properly, it will not, and so Heidegger keeps it to himself while preparing us for it. Again, simply *telling* us how to hear it will not work; it is a matter of turning us into it, gradually immersing us in it. At the time of the 'Letter', Heidegger was only just beginning this process. Thus in further marginal notes to the 'Letter' we find bits of the text translated into the 'other language', as, for instance, the word 'being' is glossed as *Ereignis* or as being.[28] And where the 'Letter' says that 'thinking is of being inasmuch as thinking, appropriated [*ereignet*] by being, belongs to being', Heidegger comments that this is 'only a pointer in the language of metaphysics'.[29] That is, the appearance of the word *ereignet* is an outpost ventured in the midst of metaphysical language, preparing us to enter into the thought of *Ereignis*.

We could only think that another language with other words was *necessary* to enter into that thought if we shared an assumption that Heidegger tries to subvert throughout his career, namely, that words and their referents are independent objects between which determinate relations can be fixed. This assumption leads us to regard words and things as if they were interchangeable, as if we might be able to substitute a word for a thing without loss, and so to suppose that we know something when we have found just the right words for it. In *Being and Time*, criticizing the notion of 'agreement' between word and thing assumed by 'the traditional concept of truth' as *adaequatio intellectus et rei*, Heidegger suggests that the relation between word and thing may be like that between a sign – a 'caution' sign, for example – and the thing it brings to our attention: 'a sign points to what is shown. Showing is a relation, but not an agreement between the sign and what is shown.'[30] The 'caution' sign on a wet floor helps the floor to show itself to us as dangerous; it presents the floor to us as wet and dangerous. A sign reading 'wet floor', meanwhile, can be said to 'agree' with some state of affairs only because the language is capable of *showing* us a wet floor, allowing a wet floor to present itself to us.

Almost two decades after the publication of *Being and Time*, in the 'Letter on "humanism"', Heidegger famously formulated the same view on the relation between word and thing in the proposition 'language is the house of being'.[31] However, Heidegger comes to back away from that proposition – in 'A dialogue on language', he calls it 'clumsy'.[32] It can all too easily give us the wrong idea, especially when we have the wrong idea about being to begin with, namely, the founding idea of metaphysics: that being is itself a being instead of a happening, and that the being of a being is its whatness, its essence. Given this assumption about being, the proposition that language is the house of being will be taken to mean that being is the *content* of language. Ideally, then, the *form* of language would mould itself precisely to the contours of that content, so that by the form of the word we would be able to recognize the being it contains. Being is, then, not presented to us *through* language but *re*-presented *by* language, which makes it easy for our use of language to become self-referential, divorced from being, phenomenologically empty, essentially meaningless.

In *What is Called Thinking?*, Heidegger writes that in such a view words are seen as 'buckets and kegs from which we scoop out a content that is there'.[33] But words, essentially, are not buckets and kegs (though they can be used that way, and indeed most of the time we do use them that way); rather 'words are wellsprings that are found and dug up in the telling, wellsprings that must be found and dug up again and again'. This passage appears in the preparation for Heidegger's etymological investigation of the word *denken*. To subvert the view of words as 'buckets and kegs', as containers which are contoured to independent, definite contents and which can substitute without loss for those contents, is one of the primary aims of Heidegger's etymological method.[34] The word is not a two-dimensional outline; the word has a historical depth which etymology digs into. Another strategy Heidegger uses to subvert our assumption of the interchangeability of words and things is his practice of making apparently drastic changes to his philosophical vocabulary, coming at the same issues again and again with different words. The former strategy shows how one word can have many meanings; the latter shows (as the English language does, latently, through its indiscriminate borrowing) how one matter can be spoken of with many words. Both show that words and things cannot map onto each other in determinate, one-to-one relationships.

Whereas the function of analysis is to 'tighten up' and narrow our sense of a term, to precisely define its limits and eliminate equivocation so that we know precisely what is at issue in a philosophical investigation, the function of etymology is rather the opposite. In the midst of and by way of contrast with his exposition of the etymological links between 'thinking' and 'thanking', Heidegger warns that 'academic philosophy' – that is, analytic philosophy, broadly speaking – 'has done its share to stunt the word', that 'conceptual definitions of terms, while necessary for technical and scientific purposes, are by themselves unfit to assure, much less advance, the soundness of language'.[35]

Of course, it is another of the later Heidegger's theses that in the current epoch, which he calls the epoch of *das Ge-Stell* or the be-setting of things by technological 'enframement', technical and scientific purposes are the ones that show themselves most strongly. But it is not only in the current epoch that words become less meaningful through their restriction for practical use. It is necessarily the case that we *almost always* do not hear what words say; when this is so, our discourse takes the form of what *Being and Time* calls *Gerede*, 'idle talk'. In *Being and Time*, Heidegger tells us that *Gerede* is the mode of discourse belonging to entangled (*verfallen*) *Da-Sein* – that is, *Da-Sein* that is caught up in the practical pursuit of its various every-day endeavours – and that *Da-Sein* is *usually* so entangled. Heidegger writes that *Gerede* 'is the mode of being of the uprooted understanding of *Da-sein*' and that 'this uprooting is constant'.[36] The translation of *Gerede* as 'idle talk' is thus somewhat misleading, since, in Heidegger's use, *Gerede* stands not only for the chit-chat we normally regard as inconsequential, but also for the talk that advances the activities we take to be of the greatest con-sequence. For instance, political debate on the most important matters is also, almost without exception, conducted in the mode of *Gerede*.

In idle talk, language does not fulfil its role of bringing us into con-tact with the being of beings: 'idle talk is the possibility of understanding everything without any previous appropriation [*Zueignung*] of the matter'; 'it omits going back to the ground [*Boden*] of what is being talked about'.[37] The 'ground' of the matter which needs to be 'appropriated' is the being of beings, and of course in our everyday lives we must almost always omit going back to it; only rarely do we have the time and space to attend to, rather than simply use, the words we speak.

Our discourse is rooted in the ground of the matter – it appropriates, makes our own, the being of beings – when we listen to what our words say: 'To think is before all else to listen'.[38] Listening to what our words say, we hear the being of beings. The word 'gives' being to us: 'we may never say of the word that it is, but rather that it gives. . . . What does it give? To go by the poetic experience and by the most ancient tradition of thinking, the word gives being'.[39] This being the case, if what is said through language changes over time, then being also changes over time. Moreover, the richer our language is, the more being will be present to us. Heidegger's etymolo-gies, in showing how words speak differently in different historical periods, demonstrate that a word can resonate more richly when its roots are still heard in it than when its roots have been forgotten.

Philosophers since Plato have held that one of the fundamental tasks of philosophy – perhaps *the* fundamental task of philosophy – is to rescue language from its everyday use and abuse. In *Being and Time*, after urging a reconception of the German *Wahrheit* (truth) on the basis of an examin-ation of the etymology and ancient usage of the Greek ἀλήθεια and λόγος,

Heidegger writes that, though this reconception would seem to fly in the face of ordinary uses of *Wahrheit*, 'in the end it is the business of philosophy to protect the *power of the most elemental words* in which *Da-sein* expresses itself from being flattened by the common understanding to the point of unintelligibility'.[40] But the statement about philosophy's business is the second part of a disjunction; the first part is this: 'we must guard against uninhibited word-mysticism'. '*Still*', he continues, philosophy's business is 'to protect the most elemental words'. We may suppose that by 'word-mysticism' Heidegger means the attitude holding that understanding something requires just that we call it by its precise name, and that we understand its name precisely – that, when we have got our words in order, we will know all we need to know. This 'word-mysticism' is part and parcel of the view that 'words are like buckets or kegs' with determinate contents, that words can substitute without loss for things. In the thrall of 'word-mysticism', we get so wrapped up in arguments about words, the relations between words and the proper uses of words, that we lose sight of the matter itself.

Of course, 'word-mysticism' is an epithet that many would find applicable to Heidegger himself, and even more so to Heideggerians who, they charge, mimic their master's vocabulary and manner of speaking without regard to its meaning or meaningfulness. The accusation is not groundless. Heidegger's strategies for subverting word-mysticism demonstrably can encourage the opposite effect. Each of the two strategies I have identified – the etymologies and the changes in vocabulary – may appear to some readers as if they are supposed to arrive at an 'authentic' language which would be adequate to being in ways that our current language is not, a language whose words we *could* substitute for things or for being itself without loss. Both strategies can become counterproductive when the assumption that words and things are independent objects fails to be shaken. When this is the case, we may take it that Heidegger is addressing different matters when he uses different sets of words, that fundamental changes in his vocabulary signal changes in what he considers to be '*die Sache selbst*', the matter itself; and we may take it that Heidegger's etymologies seek the word in an 'untainted' form, which can only be found by reaching back before the dawn of metaphysics. We may be tempted to this view of Heidegger's etymologies by, for instance, Heidegger's oft-propounded thesis on the degradation of meaning that occurred in the translation of the Greek φύσις by the Latin *natura*.[41] But the point of that thesis is not that we will have a better understanding of nature if we call it φύσις, and certainly not that we should *replace* our current definitions of 'nature' with something like 'self-blossoming emergence', which Heidegger identifies as the sense of φύσις.[42] The point is not that the words of the Greeks are more 'authentic' than our own. The language of our time, of the epoch of *das Ge-Stell*, does not speak *falsely*; language cannot speak falsely, because it always both reveals and conceals by bringing being to presence in some ways and not others. Thus we go back to the origins of our concepts in the words spoken by the Greeks not so that we can discard our current language in favour of a truer one, but so that we can recover potentialities of thought, which simultaneously means potentialities of being, that have been lost over time.

One reader who takes Heidegger to be searching for an 'authentic' language is Derrida, who writes that 'what seems . . . to be retained of metaphysics' in Heidegger's essay 'The Anaximander fragment' is 'the quest for the proper word and the unique name'.[43] As evidence, Derrida cites the following passage:

> [T]he relation to what is present that rules in the essence of presencing itself is a unique one . . . . It belongs to the uniqueness of being itself. Therefore, in order to name the essential nature of being, language would have to find a single word, the unique word.[44]

The latter sentence does indeed name a metaphysical project: matching a discrete object, defined by its essence, with the single word with which it corresponds in a one-to-one relationship and which can substitute for it without loss. Notice, however, that Heidegger speaks of the quest for the unique word for being in the subjunctive. Derrida presumes that Heidegger means to say that this quest is his own, but Heidegger continues:

> From this we can gather how daring every thoughtful word addressed to being is. Nevertheless such daring is not impossible, since being speaks always and everywhere throughout language. The difficulty lies not so much in finding in thought the word for being as in retaining purely in genuine thought the word found.

The first two sentences also appear in Derrida's quotation, but he misses the significance of the second: if being speaks always and everywhere throughout language, then the quest for the unique name for being is misguided. The task is not to *find* the word for being – the idea that there could be *the* word for anything is a metaphysical myth – because we *already have* the words through which being speaks to us. The task is rather to hear being in words when they are spoken. This is what it means to retain the word in genuine thought, what Heidegger in *Being and Time* called 'going back to the foundation of what is being talked about'.

An analogy can be made between Heideggerian etymology and Foucault's method of genealogy (even though their aims are very different). Foucauldian genealogy demonstrates how disparate elements come together in history to produce apparently stable, unitary social formations; etymology similarly demonstrates how disparate meanings can be found in the roots of apparently univocal words. For the clearest example of this we may turn to what is perhaps the clearest example of Heidegger's etymological method, namely, the explication of the three basic forms of *Sein* in *An Introduction to Metaphysics* which sets up the investigation of being in the remainder of the work. Concluding that explication, Heidegger remarks that 'etymological investigation of the word's meaning has shown that . . . what we have long called by the name of "*das Sein*" is a compromise and mixture of three different radical meanings' – according to Heidegger, these three different root meanings are 'to live, to emerge, [and] to linger or endure', belonging to the ancient roots of the German *sein/ist*, *bin/bist* and *wesen*, respectively.[45] 'None of these', Heidegger continues,

> reaches up independently to determine the meaning of the word. Mixture and effacement go hand in hand. In the combination of these two processes we find an adequate explanation of the fact . . . that the word 'being' is empty and its meaning a vapor.

That is, it is an explanation of what is *supposed* as fact by philosophers from Kant to Nietzsche to the logical positivists and their analytic heirs. Thus through etymology Heidegger aims to recover the obliterated richness of the word.

Whereas analysis 'stunts' the word in a way appropriate to technical thinking and idle talk, Heideggerian etymology expands and enriches it. As Frank Schalow writes, Heideggerian etymology 'transposes history's concerns' – that is, draws the historical meanings of a word into our present understanding of it – 'in such a way that a slightly different shade or nuance of orientation can lend new depths to what is most familiar, dramatically expanding the range of connotations'.[46] Whereas philosophical analysis is the purification and formalization of the 'compulsive exactness [of] representational [i.e. metaphysical] thought [which] turns language into an instrument of convention, omitting differences and forsaking distinctions',[47] Heideggerian etymology is its antidote, restoring to language its natural flexibility and ambiguity, fitting us together with more of being, allowing more of being to happen to us.

'Happiness' and Fittingness

If we were going to *analyse* the term 'happiness', we would want, for instance, to separate out its sense from those of related terms such as 'joy', 'pleasure', 'contentment', 'satisfaction', 'the good life' and so forth. We would be trying to determine just which phenomena count as happiness as opposed to something else, to decide which among the variety of phenomena we sometimes refer to as phenomena of happiness are properly called phenomena of happiness and which ought rather to be called something else. We would want to decide what is shared generally by 'happiness' and its related terms, and what is specific to 'happiness'; our basis for decision would be the goal of producing the greatest possible logical consistency. 'Traditionally', writes Daniel M. Haybron, 'we play the game like this: prefer whichever conception [of happiness] best matches the ordinary concept . . . . [But] the trouble is – as it often is with analysis – that the ordinary concept of happiness appears to be neither well-defined or univocal'.[48] Thus if we were analysing 'happiness', we would have to stipulate borders, more or less arbitrarily, between it and the associated terms, so as to develop a system in which the word 'happiness' would pick out *just these* phenomena, 'contentment' *just those* and so on.

Of course, if we did that, not everyone would agree with our demarcations. Some people would say, for instance, that we had 'contentment' and 'happiness' exactly reversed, or that we had made category errors such as identifying 'happiness' and 'joy' as species of the same genus when 'joy' is actually a species of the genus 'happiness'. Even people who agreed in the abstract with our demarcations would continue to use 'happiness' for the whole range of associated phenomena (joy, pleasure, etc.) – in fact, we would continue to do so ourselves – because, in actual discourse, we do not need to use 'precise' terms for our interlocutors to understand what we mean; only pedants insist on doing so. We might maintain that what we had marked out as 'happiness' was happiness in its 'philosophically significant' sense, a sense that would help us gain a deeper understanding of what happiness is, one which would in fact help us to achieve a deeper kind of happiness – but still the question would remain, on what grounds do we call it 'happiness' rather than something else? And we would have no choice but to concede that our calling it 'happiness' is, ultimately, arbitrary, because we could recognize no higher court of appeal than the prevailing intuitions of our interlocutors.

With Heideggerian etymology, the case is different. The association between word and phenomenon is not as arbitrary on the terms of

Heideggerian etymology as on those of analysis. Etymology establishes a certain claim for some phenomena to be called 'happiness' rather than 'contentment' or 'joy', even where some, or most, people's intuitions are to the contrary.[49] Heideggerian etymology assumes that the phonetic and graphic forms of words *are* significant, because the form of a word serves to collect its history. The historical senses and linkages associated with the phonetic and graphic configuration 'happiness' suggest that that configuration is particularly appropriate to certain phenomena in ways that other configurations are not. Thus etymology, like analysis, points us towards a certain field of investigation. But etymology does so in a way that is at once less arbitrary and less definite. Whereas analysis attempts to define the borders of a field of phenomena by establishing the word as a fence around it, Heideggerian etymology assumes that the word itself brings the field into view, and the more expansive our sense of the word, the more expansive the field will be.

'Happiness' is derived from the root 'hap', and thus is etymologically related to words such as 'happen' (and so like the French *bonheur* but more remotely, 'happiness' is related to time) and 'perhaps'. 'Hap', which Oxford traces to the beginning of the thirteenth century, originally means, according to Oxford: 'Chance or fortune (good or bad) that falls to anyone; luck, lot'.[50] 'Happiness' in its beginnings is thus closely tied to the relationship between the human and the divine, and to destiny – and as the relationship between the German *Geschick* (destiny) and *schicklich* (fitting) draws to our attention, that which is *destined* is also *fitting*; what I am destined to do is what it is fitting for me to do. Probing further, we find that 'hap' entered Middle English as a derivative of the Old Norse *happ*, which meant 'chance' or 'good luck'. Before the 'hap' of Middle English, Old English derived two words from the Old Norse root: *gehæplic*, meaning suitable, fitting, convenient, or orderly, and *hæplic*, meaning equal (and so 'happiness' is not only conceptually related to justice, as εὐδαιμονία is to δικαιοσύνη for Plato, but also etymologically).[51] *Happ* in turn is thought to have been derived from the prehistoric Indo-European root *kob*, meaning to suit, fit or succeed.[52] From the same root also descended the Old Slavic *kobŭ*, meaning fate, foreboding or omen.[53]

The roots of the English word 'happiness' have to do with fittingness both directly and indirectly. Clearly there is an etymological association between 'happiness' and the idea of fittingness, but clearly, also, fittingness is not of the essence of the historical group of words to which 'happiness' belongs. It should be kept in mind, however, that the purpose of the etymological excavation of the roots of 'happiness' is not to show that fittingness is its original or essential meaning. Our goal is rather to bring into view more of the 'field' that the word 'happiness' can reveal, in hopes of bringing to light an important sense of happiness lying hidden in that field.

As Richard Kraut points out, 'hap' is still a word in modern English (though it has faded out of colloquial use; Oxford marks it as archaic but not as obsolete) and it 'means chance; a hapless person is luckless; a happy turn of events is always good news'.[54] He suggests that it is 'useful' – useful, that is, for Kraut's goal of redeeming an account of happiness which is less than wholly subjectivist – 'to remind ourselves that there is a close linguistic connection between happiness and good fortune'. Because of this association between happiness and luck, John Wilson suggests that the sense of 'happiness' is closer to that of εὐτυχία, the Greek 'good luck', than to that of εὐδαιμονία.[55] As he points out, the close association between terms for what we call 'happiness' and what we call 'luck' is common in European languages: the German and French words by which we translate 'happy' – *glücklich* and *heureux* – are also those by which we translate 'lucky'. It appears only a historical quirk that our 'happy' does not still have a sense in which it is synonymous with 'lucky'. Indeed, that was one of the original senses of 'happy'. The earliest appearances of the word 'happy' are traced by the *OED* to 1340, at which time it is found to have two different senses. In the first, it means 'characterized by or involving good fortune; fortunate, lucky; prosperous; favourable, propitious'. In the second, when modifying a subject, it means 'successful in performing what the circumstances require; apt, dexterous; felicitous'; when modifying an object, it means 'characterized by fitness for the circumstance or occasion; appropriate, fitting, felicitous'.[56] In fact, the *OED* does not identify either of these senses as archaic, though it says of the first that it is 'now used only in certain collocations, in which there is an association with' either the second original sense, or the newer, and today most usual, sense: 'having a feeling of great pleasure or content of mind, arising from satisfaction with one's circumstances or condition'.

Of course, we cannot rely on the authority of the *OED*; it can only follow usage, and it may in fact lag behind usage. Are these original senses of 'happiness' still alive among contemporary English-speakers? I believe that they are. We can find the first sense preserved in such ordinary contemporary formulations as 'a happy coincidence'; the second (which is the one I wish to develop) in such formulations as 'a happy choice of words'. Of course, contemporary English-speakers might typically interpret these phrases to mean a coincidence and a choice of words which produce in somebody the *feeling* of happiness. Ninian Smart, for instance, takes such an interpretation for granted:

> [B]y some analogy we can speak of arrangements as being happy, or events. 'When is the happy event due?' we enquire of the pregnant mother. We suppose that the arrival of the child will be happy-making, and likewise a happy arrangement which in some sense or other makes the parties to it happy.[57]

However, a happy coincidence is a *fortunate* one, quite apart from whether it makes anyone *feel* happy or not – if, for instance, a used bookstore happens to have just acquired the obscure book I have just begun looking for, then it is a happy coincidence whether or not I am inclined to feel happy about it.[58]

Similarly, a happy choice of words does not necessarily make anyone happy. You may, for example, choose your words happily in directing a harsh rebuke at me, even thought it makes you miserable as well as me. A happy choice of words, which may also be called 'felicitous',[59] is one which expresses something particularly well because it is particularly apt and to the point; it is not excessive in a way that is distracting or deficient in a way that fails to bring the matter fully into view. It says exactly 'what needs to be said' in the most effective way. In other words, it is *fitting.* J. L. Austin incorporates this sense of 'happiness' into his philosophy of language when he states that a performative must be uttered under the right kind of circumstances 'if we are to be said to have happily brought off our action'.[60] When the circumstances are not right – in Austin's example, when one says 'I bet on x' after the race is over – 'the utterance is then . . . not indeed false but in general *unhappy*'. It is unhappy because it is out of place – it is not fitting.

At this point, we may wonder whether these senses of 'happy' have anything to do with *human happiness* – whether they have anything to do with the happiness that people want to achieve in their lives, or with the happiness that people 'feel' when they declare themselves happy. It may strike us that, whatever their historical links, 'happy' in the sense of 'a happy choice of words' is hardly more than a homonym of 'happy' in the sense of 'the happy life'. But it is this book's task to show that 'happy' in these two senses is not, in fact, merely homonymous, at least where deep happiness is concerned.

Kraut thinks ordinary usage indicates that there *is* a connection between 'happy' in the sense of fitting and even more ordinary human happiness. He writes:

> A happy turn of phrase is one that is just right for the context in which it occurs: if a plant is happy in a sunny window, or a dog happy on a farm,

that is because their needs and their environment are appropriately matched; and a person cannot be happy if his nature is totally unsuited for the situation in which he finds himself. In general, we speak of happiness only where there is a fit between a thing and its context. This fact is surely connected with our commonsense view that if a human being is happy then he is satisfying his major desires. Happiness requires a fit between a thing's nature and its surroundings, and since our desires form an important part of our nature, we cannot be happy unless they are fulfilled.[61]

No doubt some would argue that this is too categorically stated for ordinary usage to bear its weight. It seems likely, in any event, that it is not a necessary condition for the ascription of happiness, in ordinary usage, that we find something fitting about the situation of the person to which happiness is ascribed. But since I am not here in the business of analysing happiness, necessary conditions are not what I am looking for anyway. Roger Montague, pointing out that 'the ancestry of "happiness" is in luck, chance, fortune, the blessings of the gods', states: 'I do not think etymology illuminates the concept of happiness.'[62] Why not? Because 'it is not a necessary condition of the ascription of happiness that the man should be believed to have got there by luck or grace'. But the point of etymology, as I am deploying it here, is not to find the true meaning of 'happiness', and the point of my treatment of happiness generally is not to find necessary conditions for its ascription. Even if it were possible to discern necessary conditions for the ascription, in ordinary usage, of *any* property (which seems doubtful), what I am seeking here is not a necessary condition for the ascription of happiness to someone. I am seeking rather to bring more of the phenomenon of human happiness into view, to uncover an aspect of happiness that has been obscured.

Later Heideggerian Phenomenology

Etymology helps bring deep happiness into view by pointing out fittingness as an aspect of happiness. It reveals that happiness might, like Plato's and Aristotle's εὐδαιμονία, have some connection with fitting, both in the sense of being as it is fitting for us to be and in the sense of our fitting together with things beyond ourselves, especially with something that might be called the divine. This second sense of fitting brings us into the region of Heidegger's description of the happening of being as the mutual appropriation of being's 'in-flashing' and our 'insight' (just as the first sense brings us into the region of Heidegger's answer to the question what is fitting for human beings, to which I will turn most directly in Chapter 3). Having been brought into that region, we need to describe what we find there: we need to engage in a certain kind of phenomenology.

It is sometimes thought that, after the 'turn', Heidegger gives up his phenomenological methodology, because he gives up the project of 'fundamental ontology' that it was supposed to help carry out, in favour of a historical approach to the question of being, one which no longer inquires after the meaning of being itself but rather analyses the ways in which being manifests itself in the different epochs of history.[63] Since the metaphysical question 'what is being?' has been given up, the new task is to understand the historical contingency of what being shows up *as*, or how being is *sent* or *destined*. The later Heidegger's 'history of being' is thus taken to be akin to Foucauldian historiography, in that it is meant to loosen the grip of our current understanding of being by setting it in its historical context.

It would be a mistake, however, to consider phenomenology incompatible with the history of being. A stark division of Heidegger's work into phenomenological and historical periods can be maintained only by ignoring many of Heidegger's most important works – most particularly (for me) the lectures 'Building, dwelling, thinking' and 'The thing', and his work on poetry – as well as some of his most important concepts, including 'the fourfold', and what is arguably his *most* important concept, *Ereignis*. Towards the end of his career Heidegger remarks that though 'the age of phenomenological philosophy seems to be over', 'what is most its own in phenomenology is not a school' but 'the possibility of thinking, at times changing and only thus persisting, of corresponding to the claim of what is to be thought'.[64]

According to Heidegger in *Being and Time*, the 'phenomenon' is 'what shows itself, the self-showing, the manifest'.[65] The goal of phenomenology is to bring the phenomenon to *logos* – to that laying-out (*Aus-legung*, interpretation) in language which allows us to share with others our contact with things. Phenomenology assumes that, though phenomena are immediately available to us, and the same phenomena are available to all of us (assuming that we have our full range of sensory capacities), what is available to us *in* the phenomena is not immediately apparent. Thus phenomenology seeks not what is hidden *behind* the phenomena, as empirical methods do, but rather what is hidden *in* the phenomena themselves – what is hidden in plain view, so to speak. For a straightforwardly metaphysical phenomenology, what is hidden in the phenomena, and what it is the task of phenomenology to discover and make us aware of, are the *essences* that identify phenomena as the phenomena they are. This kind of phenomenology is a method for solving the traditional problems of philosophy, the questions 'what is knowledge?', 'what is truth?', 'what is beauty?' and so forth.

As Heidegger comes to see things, the phenomenology of *Being and Time* is metaphysical, not in pursuing the essences of particular things, but in pursuing the ground of beings in general, *das Seiende*; that ground is identified as time. Nonetheless, to say that the being of beings means the self-showing of the phenomenon is not yet metaphysical in and of itself, and indeed it is essentially this formula that Heidegger will work out for the rest of his career. However, as I have suggested, after the 'turn', Heidegger conceives of the self-showing of being in a different way, and so his phenomenological approach changes. Because Heidegger in *Being and Time* conceives being as a *temporal* self-showing, the phenomenological investigations there aim to uncover temporality. For instance, *Angst* understood phenomenologically reveals that my present includes the future possibility of my death. But after the 'turn', what is salient for Heidegger is not the ground of the self-showing, but rather the self-showing itself. The task of phenomenology now becomes to show us this self-showing, to describe the happening-to-us of being, and so to help us to overcome our oblivion of being's happening to us.

Some of the best examples of Heidegger's non-metaphysical phenomenological approach may be found in his work on poetry. Heidegger says that 'the whole point' of the dialogue between his thinking and poetry is 'to undergo an experience with language'.[66] In other words, Heidegger aims to describe in the language of thought the phenomenon that the language of the poem offers to us. It is not, however, a question of reducing that phenomenon to an essence which could then be translated into the language of thought. The ultimate concern is not 'what the poem says' but the saying itself: the goal is to bring us to see that, in poetic saying, language resumes its original function of allowing things to show themselves, allowing being to happen. Commenting on a line in a poem by Georg Trakl that says an animal's face 'freezes with blueness, with its holiness', Heidegger writes: 'blue is not an image to indicate the sense of the holy. Blueness itself is the holy, in virtue of its gathering depth which shines forth only as it veils itself'.[67] The blue of the animal's face does not refer to, indicate, or suggest a holiness which has its being elsewhere; rather, in the blue, the being of the holy happens. The blue in the poem is not an 'image' in the sense of the 'imagery' (the metaphors, similes etc.) which we are taught in school to pick out of poems, and through which, we suppose, the poem refers indirectly – in the interest of subtlety, decoration, or creating a mood – to what prose would name directly. The word 'blueness' is not a symbol that stands for 'the holy itself', where the latter is supposed to have its own independent being elsewhere. Rather, the word shows blueness to us; through the word, blueness and thereby the holy are presented to us, which is to say, their being is allowed to happen.

A different example of Heidegger's non-metaphysical phenomenology may be found in his lecture 'The thing'. That lecture sets out to investigate the thing by way of investigating *nearness*. When Heidegger asks, 'What about nearness? How can we come to know its nature?',[68] the question, since it asks about the 'nature' of nearness, appears to set us on the path of a metaphysical inquiry. But that is not the way the lecture proceeds, first of all because, according to Heidegger, 'nearness, it seems, cannot be encountered directly. We succeed in reaching it rather by attending to what is near. Near to us are what we usually call things.'[69] Thus Heidegger turns his phenomenological attention to things, asking what it is for them to be in a relation of nearness with us. In so doing he will come to interpret nearness as a way of speaking of the being of things, and our lack of nearness with things as a way of expressing the oblivion of being. The absolute remoteness of things from us as posited by metaphysics is given its ultimate formulation by Kant: ' "thing-in-itself", thought in a rigorously Kantian way, means an object that is no object for us, because it is supposed to stand, stay put, without a possible before: for the human representational act that encounters it'.[70] On this view, which Heidegger takes to be the essence of the modern, Cartesian era of metaphysics, the thing is 'out there' while I am trapped 'in here', in the representations of things conjured up in the theatre of my consciousness; between me and the thing itself there is no contact, no relation. No 'event of appropriation' occurs in which I and the thing are given over to each other – which is to say, the thing is deprived of its being.

To recover the thing from the absolute remoteness into which it is relegated by metaphysics is, then, the task of non-metaphysical phenomenology. For in fact things are not absolutely remote from us. If they were, nothing would *be* – and yet things are. The way that things are – their presencing to us – shows the error of the metaphysical conception of being. We are immersed in the evidence of this error. We do not see it because we are *too* immersed in it; we take it too much – indeed, completely – for granted. The difficulty of the task lies in this: we are told that metaphysics hides something, and so we look around for what it has hidden. But this looking around will not lead us to what is hidden, because what metaphysics hides is not a thing. What is so difficult to grasp – and yet so obvious once it is grasped – is that what we are looking for is the seeing itself, the in-flashing-in-sight of the mutual appropriation of *Ereignis*, and not any thing that can be seen.

But if the task of phenomenology is description, how can we possibly carry out a phenomenological investigation of something that is not a thing we can experience and describe? As we have seen, to understand 'nearness', Heidegger turns to an investigation of what is near, of things. Though Heidegger says that he wants 'to think being without beings', this must not be understood to mean that being is to be understood by directing our attention away from beings: being can *only* be apprehended in thought by attending to what is – to beings.[71] Our phenomenologies will never be able to point directly to being itself; all we can ever point to are beings. What we can do, however, is describe our experiences of those phenomena in which the happening of being is most apparent.

In the rest of this book, I will build my case for the view that those experiences in which the happening of being is most apparent constitute the deepest kind of human happiness. Crucial to this will be phenomenological sketches of certain situations in which the happening of being can be particularly striking – namely, in our relations with 'nature', with art, and with other human beings. These investigations will take their guidance from Heidegger's in 'The thing', insofar as deep happiness, like nearness, consists in a relationship between ourselves and things and therefore 'cannot be encountered directly'. We can never say, *this* is nearness (in Heidegger's sense). We can never say, *this* is being. Nor can we ever say, *this* is deep happiness (in the sense I will develop). What we can do instead is describe the situations in which nearness, being or deep happiness is most evident, so that, placing our readers in those situations, we might show them what we see there, and they might share our experiences.[72] If we succeed, our readers will 'see what we mean' not because we have deployed just those words which substitute for just those phenomena we want them to grasp, but because our words have brought them to look in such a way that they can see the phenomena for themselves.

As Heidegger says at the beginning of 'Time and being', 'the point is not to listen to a series of propositions, but rather to follow the movement of showing'.[73] We use the propositional form of language, but we do not limit what we hear in words to the referential function which the propositional form urges us to hear. This is what phenomenology, with its call for a return to the things themselves, asks of us: that we reject the activity of 'theory' which assumes that we understand something when we have our propositions about it in good logical order, and which assumes likewise that we understand an author when we are able to put the author's propositions in good order (i.e. the typical activity of 'commentary'). From the standpoint of phenomenology, we only understand an author when we share the experience out of which the author writes (assuming that the author does not merely string propositions together, in which case there is no possibility of genuine understanding). To develop an understanding of something, our aim as writers must be to show the thing itself to our readers in such a way as to bring about a shared experience of it. Deep happiness is not a *thing*. But this is *why* deep happiness, like being, can *only* be understood phenomenologically. Propositions always refer to things – to be a proposition is to propose something about some thing. Deep happiness, then, cannot be grasped in a series of propositions, but only in the movement of showing.

'The tuft of flowers'

We have explored Heidegger's view that language allows being to present itself to us, and that the kind of language we have available to us determines how being will present itself. We saw that Heidegger uses etymology to restore to language its multivocity, to allow words to present to us as much being as possible and to get us away from our tendency to substitute words for things, to forget being and deal only in representations of it. Poetry also often works to mitigate this tendency. Whereas we usually expect prose to surrender its meaning immediately and unequivocally (and the exceptions perhaps prove the rule: when prose deliberately does not do so, whether it is fictional prose such as Borges's or philosophical prose such as Heidegger's, we call it 'poetic'), poetic language is usually more reticent and often more multivocal. Whereas we glide quickly over prose, harvesting the ideas that we take the words to stand for, poetry invites us to slow down, to linger in its language, to listen as language speaks. What we know as poetry is the resistance of language to what Heidegger calls 'the transformation of the sign from something that shows to something that designates'[74]: the poem does not tell us *about* things, but rather shows things to us, and if all goes well, *engages* us *with* them.

But to see what the language of the poem shows, we must read the poem as a poem – we must be willing and able to slow down our reading and linger in the language. This does not come easily to most of us today; it does not come easily to me, at least. But if it did, then I would never have had the particular experiences of happiness with poetry that I will describe in this section – an experience consisting a sudden, unexpected fitting-together of the being of a being with my capacity to receive it.

Fortuitously (if not all-too-conveniently), the subject matter of Robert Frost's 'The tuft of flowers' is also a sudden, unexpected experience of the happening of being – and it is also, quite explicitly, an experience of happiness.[75] However, I have not included a discussion of 'The tuft of flowers' here because it relates to us an experience of happiness. I do not want merely to show that the poem contains the same ideas that I am trying to develop, as if to show that Frost as well as Heidegger is 'on my side'. As Heidegger warns, our purpose would be defeated if we 'reduced poetry to the servant's role as documentary proof for our thinking'.[76] In other words, we abuse poetry when we treat it purely cognitively, abstracting those ideas from it which cohere with our own views, tacitly appealing to the authority of the poet. The 'whole point' of a thoughtful engagement with poetry, Heidegger continues, is to 'undergo an experience with language'. That is, we must undergo the experience which the language of the poem allows to take place – we must experience that of being which the poem's language brings to presence for us. My experience of being through the language of 'The tuft of flowers' has provided me with some profound experiences of happiness. Through a description of one of these experiences we will hopefully develop a sense of how happiness can consist in our fitting together with being as being happens to us through language.

'The tuft of flowers' tells the story of an epiphany. The narrator, who has the task of turning the newly mown grass in a field, is surprised to discover a tuft of flowers that has been left standing by the mower who had been there that morning. Before the narrator discovers the tuft of flowers, the mower is present to the narrator in a very limited sense, as something absent. A trace of the mower is present in the effects that the mower has brought about in the world, that is, the freshly mown grass; this trace suggests the possibility that the mower is still present, leading the narrator to look for him, but the mower is gone. There is thus no particular connection between the being of the actual mower and the narrator's receptivity to being. *Someone* has been here and cut the grass, but the mower could have been anyone, and could have been any*how*. The mower, for the narrator, is only an inference, the inferred cause of an effect.

But when the narrator discovers the tuft of flowers, a connection is made – the connection is made in and through the tuft of flowers itself. The tuft of flowers is not an inert signifier but 'a message from the dawn', and what that message communicates is the being of the mower. The mower is present to the narrator, *presented* to the narrator by the tuft of flowers. And so the narrator says: 'I worked no more alone; / But glad with him, I worked as with his aid.' Before he discovered the tuft of flowers, the narrator's relationship to the mower – which, as he portrays the situation, was the main thing determining his mood – was one of unfittingness. The narrator's mood is determined by his awareness of his unfulfilled capacity to receive the being of the mower. (Turning the situation around, the mower's being is unfulfilled in its failure to be received by the mower.) But when he discovers the tuft of flowers, the being of the mower fits together with the narrator's receptivity to being – and, struck by the experience of this fitting-together, the narrator is *happy*.

My primary concern with the poem, however, is not the happiness of the narrator in the poem, but my own happiness in reading or hearing the poem. My experience of happiness with this poem that stands out most in my memory occurred while I was listening to a recording of Frost reading it. It occurred, in fact, while I was not paying full attention to the poem. Indeed, every experience of happiness that I can recall having with the poem has occurred when and indeed *due to* the fact that I had not been paying full attention to it. Not paying full attention makes it easier for something surprising to happen; it makes it all the more striking when something *comes* to our attention, when a connection is made, out of the blue.

It is a lesson of hermeneutics that we cannot pay full attention to everything at once; certainly we cannot pay full attention to a whole text at once. We cannot even understand each of the parts of a text at once, because the parts gain significance in relation to the whole. The whole, however, is constituted by the significance of the parts – hence the problem of the hermeneutic circle. But the circle is not hermetic: the work as a whole constitutes one significance-imparting horizon, but until we have a sense of the work as a whole, we import other horizons into our reading of the work, which allow us to ease our way into the circle. This is illustrated by the fact that the poem's concluding lines – ' "Men work together," I told him from the heart, / "Whether they work together or apart" ' – are famous quite independently of the particular significance imparted to them by their context in the poem. When we read the opening lines – 'I went to turn the grass once after one / Who mowed it in the dew before the sun' – for the first time, they are of course not meaningless. We know, or at least can imagine, what it is to mow and turn grass. We understand that the narrator is here now to complete a task that the mower had begun earlier. Thus we begin to develop an understanding of the situation. But we are still, for the most part, outside the situation, investigating it, piecing it together. Moreover, we do not know at this point *why* the narrator is telling us what he is telling us; we do not know why the situation is supposed to be interesting to us.

This is important for the particular experience of happiness I want to describe here. That experience relates to the middle section of the poem – the section just before we learn why the situation is interesting – in which the butterfly appears and finally draws the narrator's attention to the tuft of flowers. I had read or listened to the poem several times before this section ever *spoke* to me in the fullest sense. The significance of the butterfly is not at all apparent when it first appears, and so the lines concerning the butterfly seem, at first, like just a lull in the 'action', which picks up again after the discovery of the flowers. We do not know at first why the butterfly is 'bewildered'. We do not know at first what its 'memories grown dim o'er night' were memories of. We do not know that, when the butterfly pauses 'as where some flower lay withering on the ground', its bewildered disappointment will be overcome in the epiphany of the tuft of flowers. Indeed, the poem does not put these things – the bewildered disappointment and its overcoming – together for us; in fact, it keeps them apart by having the narrator leave the butterfly for a moment and interject, between the butterfly's disappointment and its epiphany, the couplet 'I thought of questions that have no reply, / And would have turned to toss the grass to dry.' It is easy, then, to miss the fact – at least, I did miss it, on several readings and hearings – that it is the butterfly that draws the narrator's attention to the tuft of flowers.

I had never paid enough attention to the poem to be aware of that fact. I was not at all fully paying attention to the poem when I did become aware of it. I was lying on my bed, having put on the Frost recording to help me relax. My mind was wandering, as it always does when I listen to the Frost recording (or any recording). Most times that I listen to it, the same, scattered, few lines emerge particularly forcefully. Often, the distinctive way in which Frost reads a line makes me pay attention to it. It may have been the emphatic way that Frost reads the words 'But he turned first' which finally drew my attention to the fact that it is the butterfly that leads the narrator to discover the flowers. But not just, not most importantly, to the *fact*. One can acquire facts about a poem by merely *studying* it, without ever 'undergoing an experience' with it. If I had ever studied 'The tuft of flowers', analysing it into its parts to see how they work together, I would of course have arrived very easily at the fact that the butterfly draws the narrator's attention to the tuft of flowers; the butterfly is a 'device' by which Frost advances the narrative of the poem. But the fact, per se, does not mean anything.

An artificial intelligence machine could identify and repeat the fact about the butterfly, but the fact would not mean anything to it.

What makes these lines concerning the butterfly meaningful? We might be tempted to answer: imagination. One thing we can do and which an artificial intelligence machine cannot is _imagine_ the butterfly. Having become aware of the fact that the butterfly draws the narrator's attention to the flowers, I can imagine the butterfly fluttering across the mown meadow to the flowers. And indeed, now, I do imagine that; I already have that image at the ready when I read those lines. But it was not an _image_ that struck me, that time, hearing those lines. An image may be something indicated by the words, or it may be something invoked by the words, but in any case it is something _separate_ from the words. What the words _show_, what is shown _in_ the words, is not an image – words show _things_; they are one way of showing things, and images are another. We can only form an image to match the words when the words _show_ us things, which is to say, when the words are _meaningful_ to us – the meaning must come first.

What struck me in the experience with the poem was the very _meaning of the words themselves_, which is to say, what the words bring to presence, what they _speak_. '_Die Sprache_ spricht!'[77] Language _speaks_! To speak is to say, to say something – the words, when they speak, do not just _refer to_ the butterfly; they _say the butterfly_. Not an _image_ of the butterfly but _the butterfly_ struck me. The words did not invoke for me an image of the situation; rather, they brought me _into_ the situation. But I was not in the situation as one looking on, seeing the butterfly, as in a dream. I was brought into the situation in the sense that I was brought into contact with it, it was made present to me, presented to me, not as something over against me confronting me, but as something that I _took in_ – appropriated. Thus to say that I was put into the situation _as_ the butterfly would describe something of the phenomenon, but it would still be very misleading, since it would seem to imply an act of imagination; moreover, to imagine oneself as the butterfly, though it may help one to 'feel' 'butterflyness', establishes no connection between oneself and _that butterfly_, or indeed between oneself and any _thing_ at all. What is at stake is not knowing what it is like to be a butterfly, or even knowing what it is like to be _that_ butterfly; what is at stake is not primarily a matter of _knowing_ anything at all. It is one thing to imagine a butterfly, or see an actual butterfly, or imagine oneself as a butterfly; it is another thing to be struck by the _being of_ the real or imagined butterfly, to establish that connection between oneself and it which consists in the fitting together of its being and our capacity to receive its being.

As Heidegger reminds us, to forget – whether it is being or any particular being that is forgotten – requires that we forget our forgetting. Nor can
I overcome my forgetting of being simply by 'reminding' myself of the fact
that I have forgotten being. Reminding myself of the fact does not get me
back in touch with the experience of being, and it is the experience that
I have forgotten. Reminding myself of *that* is not enough, either. Hence
the experience, when it happens, always catches us off guard. I go for a
walk beside the river, or I read Frost's poems, because I know that these
are places where I might find what I have forgotten (I can't say what it is,
but I know where to look) – I know that these are places where I might
find what I have forgotten, but I do not find what I have forgotten just by
going there. I am walking beside the river when suddenly I become aware
that the stillness of the water has caught my breath; I am listening to the
poem when suddenly my attention crystallizes from out of its dispersion as
the butterfly becomes present to me in the words – I have fit together with
its being. I have recovered what I had forgotten, and in that recovery I am
reminded that what I had forgotten is just what is most fitting for me as a
human being. So long as I dwell in this fitting-together, nothing is amiss,
nothing is wanting – I am happy.

This was not the first such experience I had had with the poem, and so I
was aware of that poem's particular capacity to occasion such experiences –
a wondrous capacity, given that it is a relatively short and quite simply written poem. Thus there was, in this experience, a double sense of *wonder*: a
sense of wonder at the sudden meaningfulness of words that had not been
meaningful to me before, and a sense of wonder at the capacity of a certain
set of words to become more and more meaningful, to allow the being of
that which is to happen to us in new ways. This sense of wonder is rooted
in the absolute mysteriousness of being's *givenness*, its arrival as a *gift*, as
something that simply *happened* to me.

Chapter 3

The Fitting-Together of Human Being and Being

Wonder

The earliest roots of this book lie in two different experiences that may be described as experiences of wonder. The first of these was an experience of wonder at being's happening to me, and the second was an experience of a perfect kind of fitting together with being which provides an exceptional opportunity for wondering at being's happening. The first – which I experienced for the first time as a young adolescent, lying idly in bed, and which recurs now and then, with equal intensity – is the shocking realization that the being of what is, its presenting itself, its happening to me, is absolutely inexplicable; that there is, in principle, no accounting for its possibility. The cognitivism of Western thought urges us, when we cannot account for the possibility of something, to consider it impossible. Under its unavoidable (if not total) sway, then, we are inclined to consider it impossible that things are – we are inclined to consider *being itself* impossible. *I* cannot avoid its sway – and so I did consider being to be impossible! It could not be *happening* – how could it? And yet, insistently, there it is, there *is*, *es gibt Sein*.

The second experience is one that I had as a child walking in the forest near my grandparents' cottage in central Ontario. It was an experience that played a large part in defining what I considered the deepest sort of happiness to be – the sort of happiness that this book seeks to describe. It is an experience that comes when the attitude of striving, of strife, that characterizes everyday life fades away and is replaced by a quiet openness to things – *Gelassenheit*, as Heidegger calls it, 'releasement', a gathered, composed, letting things happen.[1] It is an experience of being *together with* things rather than separated from and opposed to them – an experience in which, as a child walking in the forest, I would no longer look upon the trees as targets to throw rocks at, but would instead be drawn into the green of the leaves against the blue of the sky. It is an experience in which the dualism of subject and object is not *disproved* but *left behind*; the idea that the green leaves and blue sky are *re-presented* in the theatre of my consciousness, that what I am in contact with is not the things themselves but rather my own reproductions of them, simply no longer makes sense. In order for that idea to make sense, I must be detached from the experience of green leaves and blue sky; I must forget what it is like to have that experience.

At one point in his career, just when he has begun the 'turn' in his thinking, Heidegger declares that wonder should be set aside as the grounding mood (*Grundstimmung*) of philosophy. In the *Contributions*, Heidegger declares that the 'other beginning' on which he is urging thought to embark – in contrast with the metaphysical 'first beginning' launched by the Greeks – should take as its grounding mood not the 'wonder', *Erstaunen*, θαῦμα, with which Socrates says philosophy begins but what Heidegger names *Erschrecken*, which Emad and Maly translate as 'startled dismay' but which could also be translated simply as 'fright'.[2] 'Startled dismay', for Heidegger, 'lets man return to face *that* a being *is*, whereas before a being was for him just a being'. What is startling is the sudden apprehension of the 'abandonment of being', *Seynsverlassenheit* (a concept that will be discussed in the next chapter) – that 'being [*Seyn*] has withdrawn from beings'.[3] It is dismaying partly because in that apprehension one becomes aware of one's own involvement in *Seynsverlassenheit*, and of how extraordinarily difficult it would be to overcome *Seynsverlassenheit* in general. The difficulty is apparent when one tries to convey to others '*that* a being *is*', that being *could* be forgotten (or that we could be in a relation of mutual abandonment with it), and that our typical ways of being in the world betray that we *have* forgotten it, that we have abandoned being and being has abandoned us. Nonetheless, for me, that dismay is founded in wonder; the abandonment of being is dismaying because being itself – *that* being *is* – is a wonder.

Heidegger writes that *Erschrecken* 'can be most appropriately clarified by contrasting it with the grounding mood of the first beginning, with *wonder*'.[4] But the English word 'wonder' has two senses, as indeed does the Greek θαῦμα. We may refer to these as, first, 'wondering-at' (or 'being filled with wonder'), and second (which is a later derivative of the first, in both English and Greek), 'wondering-what'. The German *Erstaunen*, or 'astonishment', unlike *Wunder* (which, for this reason, is likely a better translation for θαῦμα), has only the first sense. When I see the northern lights or hear someone playing the piano, I may, on one hand, wonder *at* them, 'filled with wonder' by them. On the other hand, I may, in a scientific mood, wonder *what causes* the northern lights, or what the mechanisms are by which the

piano and pianist combine to produce the sounds I hear; in a philosophical mood, I may wonder *what are* the colours of the northern lights, or the
sound of the piano, or my emotional responses to them – even my wonder
at them itself.

The first kind of wonder often prompts the second: I may wonder what
causes that which I wonder at, and look for an *explanation*. But the first
kind of wonder is lost in the second. When I look for an explanation of
that which I had wondered at, I leave behind not only my being filled with
wonder in the experience of the phenomenon, but also the phenomenon
itself. And the results of the second kind of wonder often make the first
harder to come by. Though I may still be (and in fact I am) filled with wonder at the northern lights after I know that they are caused by magnetic
particles discharged from the sun reacting in the Earth's ionosphere, once
I can explain them in that way – once I can *reduce* them to causal physical
processes – I am made free to ignore them. They are not, at any rate, 'simply wonderful' any longer. 'The northern lights? They are just . . .'.[5]

And not only the physical sciences have this effect. Metaphysical philosophy also aims at the reduction of multiple phenomena to a unitary essence.
When Socrates asks Meno what virtue is, he is looking for a single answer,
not the many supplied by Meno. If we know what virtue is, and, on the
basis of that knowledge, we come to know how to make people virtuous,
then virtuous people are no longer 'a wonder'. Because no such knowledge
can be found in the *Meno*, virtue is indeed, at the end of the dialogue,
still a wonder – an inexplicable, unteachable gift from the gods. It is still a
wonder – but as long as we take up the attitude of the metaphysical philosopher towards it, we will not be filled with wonder at it.

The Socratic dictum that 'philosophy begins in wonder' comes to us from a
passage in the *Theaetetus*. Having enumerated some Protagorean paradoxes
concerning relations among things (e.g. one may become 'smaller' without
decreasing in size if the person to whom one's size is compared grows),
Socrates says to Theaetetus, 'you follow me, I take it, . . . for I think you are
not new at such things'.[6] Indeed Theaetetus is not; he replies that he wonders extraordinarily (ὑπερθυῶς ὡς θαυμάζω) when he thinks of them – in
fact, he says, they make him feel as if he will black out (σκοτοδινιῶ) – and
Socrates remarks that 'this feeling of wonder [τὸ πάθος, τὸ θαυμάζειν]
shows that you are a philosopher, since wonder is the only beginning of
philosophy'. Theaetetus describes this wonder as something that would
make him black out – translators also have rendered σκοτοδινιῶ as 'makes
my head swim' and 'makes me dizzy'[7] – and Socrates calls it a 'feeling'
(πάθος). Thus it seems more akin to our first sense of wonder than to our
second. But this 'feeling' of wonder is produced by the difficulty of solving

logical paradoxes. Theaetetus may be, to some extent, filled with wonder at the paradoxes, but more likely, if he is filled with wonder at anything it is their resistance to being solved; what overwhelms him is his wondering what their solutions are. It seems likely that Plato is conscious of the double sense of 'wonder' and is playing on the ambiguity in this passage.

I might say of my experience in which I was suddenly overwhelmed by the inexplicability of being's happening to me that it made my head swim with wonder like Theaetetus's experience with the paradoxes. Unlike Theaetetus, however, I knew that there was no solution, and that in fact there was not even a problem. If there were a problem, the problem would be to account for the possibility of being, but it is immediately evident (as long as we keep being in sight and it does not fall back into oblivion) that there is no possible solution to such a problem. 'Because God makes it so' is not even the beginning of a solution, because there is no accounting for what God could do to make it so. We could imagine God doing all the things that we think are necessary for beings to be – bringing things forth from the void and imparting to each its form and matter on one hand, giving us the sort of physiology that endows us with our perceptual capacities on the other – but we would be no closer to accounting for the happening-to-us of the being of things. Wonder at the happening of being therefore is a unique wondering-at in that it defies transformation into a wondering-what.

Wondering at beings, however, is always susceptible to transformation into some kind of wondering-what. If the proposition that philosophy begins in wonder is ambiguous between the two kinds of wonder when it is made by Socrates, Aristotle makes it unequivocal when he begins the *Metaphysics* with a statement that, in one representative translation, is rendered 'all human beings by nature desire to know'.[8] The word translated by 'know' is εἰδέναι, which is related to Plato's εἶδος and ἰδέα, and which more literally means to see – as we would say, to look into. And what do human beings desire to look into – what is it that philosophy will help them to see? At the beginning of the *Physics*, Aristotle declares that 'we conceive ourselves to know about a thing when we are acquainted with its ultimate causes [αἴτια] and first principles [ἀρχάς]'.[9] Again in the *Metaphysics*, we find that the kind of knowledge we are to seek is knowledge of causes, as is evident when Aristotle judges τέχνη – know-how founded on theory, usually translated as 'science' or 'art' but in this context fittingly translated as 'technology' – superior to ἐμπειρία – know-how founded on experience – because 'the experienced know the that [ὅτι], but not the why [διότι]; but the technologists [τεχνίτας] know the why and the cause [αἰτίαν]'.[10] With Aristotle, then, it is clear that wondering-what, and not wondering-at, is the real beginning of philosophy.[11]

Wondering-what, as the essence of metaphysics, is the kind of wonder that thinking must leave behind, if it is to think being as *Ereignis*.

Wonder, in the sense of wondering-at, *is* an attunement on the basis of which being can be thought as the mutual appropriation of being and human being. However, not all wondering-at will serve as the basis for that thinking – indeed, most will not. Aristotelian contemplation of divine things, for instance, even if it is a wondering-at rather than a wondering-what, still is a wondering concerning *beings*, not a wondering concerning *being*. Whenever we wonder at such mundane marvels as the speed of a new computer – a wondering-at which always has the potential to turn into a wondering-what – we are wondering concerning beings rather than being. Indeed, Heidegger himself does not differentiate between wondering-at and wondering-what, and considers only the Greeks' way of wondering-at being – their way of wondering at being's being present *before* them, rather than at being's presenting itself *to* them – which has them 'step back' from being, regard being as a being, and wonder, metaphysically, what being is.[12] What we are looking to achieve, with Heidegger, is a 'turn' out of the wondering-what that characterizes Western thinking – not only the thinking of philosophers – and into a wondering-at concerning not some particular beings, or even being in the metaphysical sense of beings-as-such-and-as-a-whole, but rather being itself in its happening to us. Such wondering-at is not identical to deep happiness, but it is an aspect of it.

'Startled dismay' results from the recognition of the damage initiated by philosophy's first beginning in wondering-what.[13] 'Startled dismay' is a recognition of what has slipped away and may be lost altogether, that is, that beings *are*. We may understand the wondering at being that is an aspect of deep happiness as the positive inversion of this startled dismay: deep happiness points us towards being not as what has been lost but as what may be found. This happiness, I thus propose, is the grounding mood for the thinking of being: when our fitting together with being is not subverted, when we dwell in being's happening to us, we are deeply happy; when we are happy, there is the opportunity that our happiness will manifest itself in the apprehension of being itself in our wondering at being. Opportunities abound: the trick is to grasp them for what they are.

The Essence of Human Beings

If deep happiness has something to do with what is fitting for human beings, and we want to see where deep happiness lies, then we need to know what is fitting for human beings. But if we want to know what is fitting for human beings, then we need to know what human beings are. We need, in other words, to know the essence of human being. This is, on the face of it, a metaphysical question, but it is one that Heidegger grapples with, both before and after the 'turn'. In *Being and Time*, Heidegger famously declares that 'the "essence" of *Da-sein* lies in its existence',[14] and it is partly in response to the Sartrean appropriation of that slogan (transformed into 'existence precedes essence') that Heidegger returns to the question of the human essence in the 1947 'Letter on "Humanism"'.[15] Heidegger writes in the 'Letter' that 'the opposition between *existentia* and *essentia* is not what is at issue [in *Being and Time*], because neither of these metaphysical deter-minations of being, let alone their relationship, is yet in question'.[16] This seems perplexing, given that in *Being and Time* Heidegger had written not only that 'the whatness (*essentia*) of [*Da-sein*] must be understood in terms of its being (*existentia*) insofar as one can speak of it at all',[17] but also that 'the priority of "*existentia*" over *essentia*' is one of 'the two characteristics of *Da-sein*' (along with 'always-being-mine').[18] However, these passages are littered with scare-quotes and qualifications: *insofar as one can speak of the essence of Da-Sein at all* – which, of course, one cannot, in the usual meta-physical senses of 'essence' – its 'essence' lies in its 'existence'. Heidegger leaves no doubt that the 'essence' spoken of is not an essence of the usual metaphysical sort when he writes that 'the characteristics to be found in [*Da-sein*] are . . . not objectively present "attributes" of an objectively pre-sent being which has such and such an "outward appearance" [*Aussehen*, Heidegger's word for Plato's εἶδος], but rather possible ways for it to be'.[19]

What does it mean to say that the 'essence' of *Da-Sein* lies in its 'exist-ence'? In *Being and Time* Heidegger means by the 'existence' of *Da-Sein* its temporal transcendence towards being, which he will later emphasize by rendering the word as *ek-sistenz*, bringing out its relationship with our temporally 'ecstatic' nature.[20] Heidegger goes on to explain that his 'ek-sistence' is different from metaphysical existence because the latter is con-ceived in terms of actuality: on metaphysical terms, essence determines what might be, while existence comprises what actually is. But the tem-poral ek-sistence of human being is a self-transcendence towards future possibilities.

During and after the period of the 'turn', the concept of essence takes on heightened importance for Heidegger, as he often inquires into the essence, *Wesen* – without scare-quotes – of some kind of thing, including artworks, truth, freedom and nations as well as human beings, developing his own sense of *wesen* as a verb, indicating that the essence of a thing is not something it *has* but something that *happens* in its presenting itself to (*an-wesen*) us, and that happens differently in different epochs of being. Thus in many passages we find peculiar phrases of the form 'such-and-such essences . . .'. Heidegger's English translators often translate Heidegger's *wesen* with the verb 'to presence', but I find 'to essence' preferable for several reasons: it avoids confusion with Heidegger's *anwesen*; it captures the deliberate strangeness of Heidegger's use of *wesen*, which is designed to make us rethink the idea of essence; and it captures the sense that something's 'essencing' is not only its manifestation but its manifestation *as* something, which links Heidegger's sense to the conventional one.[21]

As we saw in the last chapter, in the 'Letter', Heidegger is translating his own peculiar vocabulary, which he had begun to develop in the mid-1930s in order to express the thought of *Ereignis*, into the familiar terms of metaphysical philosophy. Thus the 'Letter' mediates not only between Heidegger's earlier and later thought – the former of which, for the letter's specific addressee as well as its general audience, *is* Heidegger – but also between Heidegger's new kind of thinking and the traditional problems of metaphysical philosophy. The 'Letter' is forced to speak the language of metaphysical philosophy insofar as it engages with a question – 'how can we restore meaning to the word "humanism"?' – which is posed in metaphysical terms. For Heidegger, to answer this question is to risk falling into a metaphysical trap, because 'every determination of the essence of the human being that already presupposes an interpretation of being without asking about the truth of being' – that is, to be under the sway of an epochal destining of being without attending to how being is sent to us, how it happens – 'is already metaphysical'.[22] Thought non-metaphysically, the essence, *Wesen*, of human being is an 'essenc*ing*', *wesen*; it is something that happens.

What, then, is the essence of the human for the later Heidegger? As for the Heidegger of *Being and Time*, the essence of the human lies in its relation with being. But being is now thought differently, and so the temporally transcendent ek-sistence of human being is no longer considered to be what is most fundamental in the human relation with being. What is most fundamental about being for the later Heidegger is that it happens to us. In keeping with this notion, what is most fundamental about human being for the later Heidegger is that it allows for being to happen; it is the relationship itself, without which being would not happen, that is important.

Three words come up again and again in Heidegger's characterization of the human essence in texts from the 'Letter' to the 1957 lecture 'The principle of identity'. These are *gehören*, to belong, *hören*, to hear or to listen, and *entsprechen*, to correspond or to respond: human beings are those who *belong* to being, who *listen* to being and *respond correspondingly* to what they have heard. For example, in the 'Letter', Heidegger writes:

> Thinking is the thinking of being. The genitive says something twofold. Thinking is of being inasmuch as thinking, appropriated by being, belongs [*gehört*] to being. At the same time thinking is of being insofar as thinking, belonging to being, listens [*hört*] to being.[23]

Similarly in 'On the question of being':

> Presencing ('being') is, as presencing . . . a presencing directed toward the human essence, insofar as presencing is a call [*Geheiß*] that on each occasion calls upon the human essence. The human essence as such is hearing [*hörend*], because the essence of human beings belongs [*gehört*] to the calling of this call, to the approach of presencing.[24]

And finally in 'The principle of identity':

> Man's distinctive feature lies in this, that he, as the being who thinks, is open to being, face to face with being; thus man remains related to being and so corresponds [*entspricht*] to it. Man *is* properly this relationship of corresponding [*Entsprechung*], and he is only this . . . . A belonging [*Gehören*] to being prevails within man, a belonging which listens [*hört*] to being because it is appropriated [*übereignet*] to being.[25]

Let us examine first Heidegger's comment in the 'Letter' that in the phrase 'thinking of being', 'the genitive says something twofold'. This means that while the thinking of being is *our* thinking of being, it is also *being's* thinking, with us. Human thinking is being's thinking itself. As the ones who speak, we are the ones who *can* carry out the thinking of being, being's thinking itself, which is to say, its manifestation in language. This does not mean that being is an agent using us as its instruments; it means that in thinking we say how being *is to us*, which is not determined by any agency that we can account for. Thus, later on in the 'Letter', Heidegger writes, invoking terms we encountered in our discussion of his interpretation of Anaximander, that 'thinking builds upon the house of being' – that is, language – 'in which the jointure [*Fuge*] of being in its destinal unfolding, enjoins [*verfügt*] the essence of the human being in each case to dwell in the truth of being'.[26] Recall that in his interpretation of Anaximander

in *Basic Concepts*, Heidegger writes that 'enjoinment [*Verfügung*] is being':
things *are* when we are enjoined by them, related to them, fit together
with them, a notion which is already present, in the same terms, in the
Contributions: '*Ereignis* names *Seyn* in thinking and grounds *Seyn*'s essencing
in its own jointure [*Gefüge*].'[27] In the passage we have cited from the 'Letter',
Heidegger is saying that this fitting together with things comes about
through language. Without the connection that language forges between
us and things, allowing them to present themselves to us in a certain way,
there could be no 'essencing' of any thing; the thing would not come to
presence as anything.

Again in the 'Letter', Heidegger says that 'thinking in its saying merely
brings the unspoken word of being' – which we hear, *hören*, in our belonging, *gehören*, to being – 'to language . . . . Being comes, lighting [*lichtend*]
itself, to language. It is perpetually under way to language'.[28] In the previous paragraph, we have seen how Heidegger speaks of being presenting
itself to us in its epochal destinings. Perpetually under way *towards* language, being is *fulfilled* when it arrives in language. Language allows *beings*
to be, to manifest themselves as what they are under the sway of a certain
epoch of being, to 'essence'. But as Heidegger says in 'The turning', language also allows *being itself*, being in the sense of *Ereignis*, to 'essence':

> The human *essence* belongs [*gehört*] to the essence of being [*Seyns*] – inas-
> much as being's [*Seyns*] essence needs man's essence, in order to remain
> kept safe [*gewahrt*] as being [*Sein*] in keeping with its own essence in the
> midst of beings, and thus to essence *as* being [*Seyn*].[29]

Not only do beings need the human belonging, listening and responding to being in order to be what they are; *being itself* needs the human
essence in order to manifest itself *as* itself. We may understand this point
by thinking of the difference between humans and non-human animals.
On one level, we may say that non-human animals relate to things, but only
humans relate to things *as* the things they are; on another level, we may say
that non-human animals are immersed in being as we are, but 'captivated'
by beings so that they cannot *recognize* being as such: only to humans can
being manifest itself *as* itself (though we are *mostly* captivated by beings as
well); only humans are capable of recognizing (the absolute mystery) that
Es gibt Sein.[30]

Es gibt Sein is the phrase Heidegger uses to avoid saying that 'being is'.
Heidegger points out in the 'Letter' that already in *Being and Time* he had
consciously avoided saying 'being is', *Sein ist*; only a being is, and being is

not a being.[31] Instead he had used the formula *Es gibt Sein,* an idiomatic expression which has the sense of 'there is being' but which, to avoid reactivating the problem the expression is designed to get around, is literally translated into English as 'it gives being'. For Heidegger, who is always attentive to what words say, to say *Es gibt Sein* is to invoke the question, what is the 'it' that gives being? The 'it' that gives being cannot itself be a being – the idea that being must be given by some thing that grounds being is the fatal mistake of metaphysics. But if no thing can be the giver of being, what can give being?

What is no thing? *Being* is no thing, nothing, as Heidegger said in 'What is metaphysics?'[32] And indeed, in the 'Letter' Heidegger says that 'the "it" that . . . "gives" is being itself'.[33] And what about the 'giving'? Heidegger continues: 'The "gives" names the essence of being that is giving, granting its truth' – that is, happening to us, and in happening to us, disclosing, revealing, manifesting, presenting itself, under the sway of an epochal destining. Heidegger continues: 'the self-giving into the open' – that is, into the 'clearing' provided by human being, in which being 'lights up' in its 'in-flashing' – 'along with the open region itself' – that is, human being with its receptivity to being, its 'in-sight' – 'is being itself'. The paradoxical nature of this formulation is due to the fact that, in the language of metaphysics, 'being' names something other than us – being is object to our subject. But what Heidegger is saying is that being is *not* other than us; human being 'belongs together' with being in such a way that neither being nor human being can be without the other.

Hence the later Heidegger's discussions of the human essence always arrive at the suggestion that it is actually misleading to speak of a *relation* between human being, on one hand, and being, on the other. We see this already in the text where Heidegger first intensively works through his post-'turn' conception of being, the *Contributions:* 'talk of a relation of *Da-Sein to* being is misleading, insofar as this suggests that being essences "for itself" and that *Da-Sein* takes up the relating to being . . . . Being needs *Da-Sein* and does not essence at all without this *Ereignis*'.[34] In the 'Letter', Heidegger gestures towards this thought with these words: 'how – provided we really ought to ask such a question at all – how does being relate to [human] ek-sistence? Being itself is the relation to the extent that it . . . gathers to itself and embraces ek-sistence'.[35] In this sense, then, there is no relation between human being and being; as was already indicated in, for instance, the statement that 'enjoining is being', being itself is the 'relation', so to speak. Being as this 'relation' is the *turning* that was discussed in Chapter 2, the reversibility between our experience of being and being itself, between, as Heidegger puts it in 'The turning', our 'insight', *Einblicken*, into being, and being's 'in-flashing', *Einblitzen*, into us: experience and being, 'in-sight' and 'in-flashing', are not two *different* things, but two sides of the same coin.

Are human being and being then *identical?* Heidegger says in 'On the question of being' that 'we cannot then even continue to say that "being" and "the human being" "are" the same in the sense that *they* belong together, for when we say it in *this* way, we continue to let both subsist independently'.[36] On the other hand, in 'The principle of identity', we see Heidegger's thinking move in the opposite direction, from the idea that human being and being are identical, to their belonging together. There he begins with Parmenides's saying τό γὰρ αὐτο νοεῖν ἐστίν τε καὶ εἶναι, commonly rendered 'thinking and being are the same', interpreting it as follows: 'thinking and being belong together in the same and by virtue of this same'.[37] This 'same' is being in the sense of *Seyn*; it is being in the sense that Heidegger, in the 'Letter', says that being itself is the relation between being-as and human being: human being and being belong together in the turning, the in-sight and in-flashing, that unites them. Heidegger's interpretation of Parmenides's saying leads to the explication, cited above, of the human belonging, listening and corresponding to being.

Being and human being need each other. The essence of each lies in the other; each, we may say, essences towards the other, fulfilling itself in its fitting-together with the other. In 'On the question of being', Heidegger writes that 'we always say *too little* of "being itself" when, in saying "being", we omit its essential presencing *toward* [*An-wesen*] the human *essence* and thereby fail to see that this essence itself is part of "being" ',[38] and the same is true of human being: human being essences towards being in opening itself to receive the essencing of being. In 'Time and being', Heidegger puts it this way:

> If man were not the constant receiver of the gift given by the 'it gives presence', if that which is extended in the gift did not reach man, then not only would being remain concealed in the absence of this gift, not only closed off, but man would remain excluded from the scope of: it gives being. Man would not be man.[39]

The Gathered Four, the Divinities and the Holy

I noted in the Introduction that Heidegger employs the b̶e̶i̶n̶g̶ device for the same reason that he uses the archaic spelling *Seyn*, namely, to show that being must be thought in a non-metaphysical way. Heidegger writes in 'On the question of being' that this device has the role of 'preventing the almost ineradicable habit of representing "being" as standing somewhere on its own that then on occasion first comes face-to-face with human beings'.[40] But the cross through the word *Sein* has a deeper significance for Heidegger: 'it points . . . toward the four regions of the gathered four and their being gathered in the site of this crossing through'.[41]

Heidegger here provides a reference to his lecture 'The thing', where he gives his most sustained treatment of his concept of *das Geviert* or *die Vierung*, 'the gathered four' or 'the fouring',[42] consisting of mortals, divinities (*die Göttlichen*), earth, and sky. There, with the help of an etymological investigation into the word *ding* (which is etymologically related to the English 'thing'), we find the thing described as a *gatherer*: mortals, divinities, earth and sky, the four 'regions' of being, are gathered in the thing, by the 'thinging' of the thing. In its gathering of these four, the thing allows being to happen: the thing is thus the site of the crossing through of being; the thing is the joining in the middle of the cross, where the four fit together in mutual appropriation.

Elsewhere, of course, the *Ereignis* of being is described as taking place between being and human being; here, *Ereignis* is described as having four constituents rather than two. In addition to human beings, there are earth, sky and divinities. The interplay between human being and the divine is particularly important for my purposes here, as it will return us to the essence of εὐδαιμονία, having a good δαίμων, which I interpreted in Chapter 1 as consisting in a fitting relationship between the mortal and the divine. I will begin my examination of the gathered four by considering Heidegger's description of human beings as 'mortals', which will complement much of the discussion in the last section.

The paragraph devoted to the mortals, in the section of 'The thing' that outlines each of the regions of the gathered four, is noteworthy for the fact that it is the only place in the lecture that the word *Sein* appears. There, Heidegger says that mortals, as opposed to non-human animals, are those who have death before them, and death, he says, 'is the shrine of the nothing, that is, namely, of that which in every respect is never something that is merely a being, but which nevertheless essences, namely as being [*Sein*] itself'.[43] Human death is the possibility of there being nothing, no-thing – in this case, the English 'nothing' makes the point more strikingly than the German *Nicht*. Without the mortal, one of the regions of the gathered four would be missing, and so the thing's gathering would be impossible, which is to say that there could be no thing; there would be no site at which being takes place. There would be *nothing*; nothing would *be*. When the sending of being is not fulfilled in its being received by human being, no thing is.

Just as, without the mortal, there could be no thing that allows for the happening of being, so also without any of the other three. Earth, which Heidegger describes as 'the building bearer',[44] provides for the materiality of things. Sky, which Heidegger says

> is the sun's path, the course of the moon, the glitter of the stars, the year's seasons, the light and dusk of day, the gloom and glow of night, the clemency and inclemency of the weather, the drifting clouds and the blue depth of the ether,[45]

provides for the animation of things, their growing with and into, the air and sunlight, as well as their developing and decaying according to the rhythms of the changing skies.

What about the divinities? When Heidegger describes *die Göttlichen*, in both 'The thing' and 'Building dwelling thinking', he invokes two other divine elements alongside *die Göttlichen*: *der Gott* and *die Gottheit*, translated by Hofstadter as 'the god' and 'the godhead'. In 'The thing', Heidegger writes: '*Die Göttlichen* are the beckoning messengers of *die Gottheit*. Out of its hidden sway, *der Gott* emerges in his essence, which removes him from any comparison with that which presences [*das Anwesenden*].'[46] In 'Building dwelling thinking', an almost identical passage appears; the first sentence – '*Die Göttlichen* are the beckoning messengers of *die Gottheit*' – is the same; the second has 'holy sway' instead of 'hidden sway', and says: '*der Gott* appears in his presence or withdraws into his concealment. Out of the holy sway of *die Gottheit, der Gott* appears in his presence or withdraws into his concealment.'[47] In order to understand the role of *die Göttlichen* in the gathered four we need to understand what *die Gottheit* and *der Gott* are in distinction from *die Göttlichen*.

This is a question of not merely scholarly interest. Heidegger is trying to *show* us something by describing things in terms of the gathered four. What Heidegger is trying to show us is something that is there for us to see, and that this is so is confirmed by the fact that one does not need Heidegger to see it. Below, I will try to show that what Heidegger describes is also seen and shown by Isak Dinesen in her short story 'Babette's feast'. 'Babette's feast' concerns earth, sky, mortals and, especially, divinities – and not just divinities, but also divinity itself, and the gods in whose form divinity reveals itself. As a work of art, it is an important complement to Heidegger's description. Where Heidegger's description gives us to *think about* the happening of being in the gathered four, Dinesen's story brings us more sensuously into the *experience* of it.

Heidegger describes *die Göttlichen* as 'the beckoning messengers of the godhead'.[48] 'Godhead' is an obscure word to secular ears, and a potentially misleading one, but if heard correctly, a very appropriate and illuminating one. 'Godhead' is closely etymologically related to *Gottheit*; the suffix-head, in this instance, is derived from the same proto-Germanic root as the German –*heit* and also the more common English-hood.[49] It would be an all-too-easy mistake to hear 'godhead' as akin to, for instance, 'fountainhead'. The godhead is not the *source* of god-ness as the fountainhead is the source of the fountain's water; rather, the godhead is god-ness, divinity, or in the word Heidegger uses in his commentaries on Hölderlin, 'the holy', *das Heilige*, itself. The divinities beckon us, they draw us, to the holy. Recalling the link Heidegger draws in the *Parmenides* lectures between δαίμων and δαίω, such that the δαίμων is one who points and shows, we can say that Heidegger's divinities are δαίμονες.[50]

The roles of the divinities and the god are similar, but they are not precisely the same. In 'The thing', after he says that 'the divinities are the beckoning messengers of the godhead', Heidegger continues: 'out of the hidden sway of the godhead the god appears in his essence'.[51] The divinities beckon us *to* the godhead, *out of* which the god appears; the god is the essencing, the manifestation in a particular way, of the godhead. The god does not *create* the godhead. The godhead is not a function of, dependent on, the god, as it is held to be in the monotheistic religions; the godhead, the holy, is 'higher' than the god. In his commentary on Hölderlin's 'As when on a holiday . . .', Heidegger describes the relation between 'the god' and 'the holy'. The poet needs to be inspired by the holy, and for this to occur,

> someone higher, who is nearer to the holy and yet still remains beneath it, a god, must throw the kindling lightning-flash into the poet's soul. Thus the god takes upon himself that which is 'above' him, the holy, and brings it together into the sharpness and force of the unique ray through which he is 'allotted' to man, in order to bestow it.[52]

The god is our channel to the holy, reminding us of and drawing our attention to the holy. When we *worship* a god in the proper spirit, then, the holy is made present to us, and our worship is our way of responding to the holy as holy. The god is the *shape* through which the divine becomes present to us; the god shows divinity to us (recalling Heidegger's link between the

Greek homonyms θέα and θέα, 'goddess' and 'view') in a certain aspect. The shape the god takes is influenced by the community to which the god emerges; in different cultures, the god may take the shape of the supreme law-giver or warrior or earth-spirit. But whatever shape it takes, the essence of the god is to manifest the divine to human beings. This means that when the god is for us only in the aspect of law-giver, or only in the aspects of law-giver and creator, then the god is deprived of its god-ness.

In the 'Letter', the *Parmenides* lectures, and the Hölderlin essay, δαίμονες and θεοί are thought of as the same insofar as they are both beings which bring us into contact with the holy. In the texts where Heidegger speaks in terms of the gathered four, *die Göttlichen* and *der Gott* are thought of as different insofar as *die Göttlichen* bring us the message of the holy, beckoning us to the holy, while *der Gott* is that figure through which the holy *as* the holy is manifest to us. Their roles are different, but in essence they are still the same: they both bring us to attend to the holy.

What is the holy? In order to answer this question, let us examine the role of the divinities in the example Heidegger uses – that of a jug and the water or wine poured out of it – to describe the gathering of the four in the thing. Heidegger says that, in addition to the jug's pouring to quench thirst,

> the jug's gift is at times also given for consecration. If the pouring is for consecration, then it does not still a thirst. It stills and elevates the celebration of the feast . . . . The outpouring is the libation poured out for the immortal gods . . . . In the giving of the consecrated libation, the pouring jug essences as the giving gift.[53]

A little further on, Heidegger says:

> In the gift of the outpouring that is drink, mortals stay in their own way. In the gift of the outpouring that is a libation, the divinities stay in their own way . . . . In the gift of the outpouring, mortals and divinities each dwell in their different ways. Earth and sky dwell in the gift of the out-pouring. In the gift of the outpouring, earth and sky, divinities and mortals dwell *together all at once*.[54]

In pouring out drink, the jug gathers mortals. In pouring out consecrated drink, the jug gathers divinities. Divinities are *present* in the consecrated drink, beckoning us towards the holy. But again, what is the holy? When it pours the drink in which we are beckoned to the holy, 'the pouring jug essences' – it presents itself to us as what it is – 'as the giving gift' – not only as giver, but as given, as presented to us. Beckoned to the holy, we are beckoned to the jug's being presented to us – to its *being* (in the sense of *Seyn*). The holy, which is 'above' the god, is the absolute mystery which we can only revere, never explain or understand; it can only 'still' us. The being of the thing is this absolute mystery: the holy is being itself.

Wherever we are beckoned to attend to being, divinities are present. But these divinities should not be thought of as 'super-persons', so to speak, as 'gods' and 'angels' have typically been thought of: divinities consist in whatever beckons us to the holy, to being. Whatever beckons us to the holy, connects us with the holy, is a δαίμων. And when the δαίμων succeeds in forging a fitting relation between us and being, we are εὐδαίμων.

'Babette's feast'

I must begin this section with a warning and a plea. I am going to 'give away' much of 'Babette's feast'. Of course, the 'content' of the story does not begin to exhaust its importance or its greatness as a work of art, but it is one way of the story's being, and it would be a shame if the reader did not have the chance to receive the story's being in its fullness all at once. Of course, as we have seen with 'The tuft of flowers', this may not be necessary to have an experience of deep happiness in fitting together with the being of a work of art; moreover, the threads of 'Babette's feast' are so subtly woven together that it rewards revisitation again and again. Nevertheless, I implore the reader to read the story, or to see the wonderful film adaptation, before reading this section.

'Babette's feast' takes place in the late nineteenth century in a small Danish community whose members belong to a devout and ascetic Lutheran sect founded by the late father of two of the story's main characters, Martine and Philippa. Babette is a refugee from Paris who fled after the rout of the Commune, and who now works as housemaid and cook for Martine and Philippa. The occasion of the story is the coincidence of Babette's winning 10,000 francs in a lottery and the hundredth anniversary of Martine and Philippa's father's birth, for which Babette implores the sisters to be allowed to cook 'a real French dinner'.[55] The sisters, who eat only the simplest food, are disturbed by Babette's request, but accede to it because it is the only thing that she has ever asked of them since they took her in, and they believe that she will soon return to Paris with her new wealth.

The bulk of 'Babette's feast' is taken up with backstory concerning the routes by which the feast's elements converged. One of the main elements is Lorens Loewenhielm, a general when he is a guest at the feast, who had been a young lieutenant when he had first come to Martine and Philippa's village, long before Babette, sent there by his father to learn self-control from the ascetics. He was indeed shown a vision of life free from worldly distractions, but the vision was not in the examples of asceticism; it was the vision of Martine: 'at this one moment', when he first laid eyes on her,

> there rose before his eyes a sudden, mighty vision of a higher and purer life, with no creditors, dunning letters or parental lectures, with no secret, unpleasant pangs of conscience and with a gentle, golden-haired angel to guide and reward him.[56]

This, reminiscent of what the *Symposium* says about Ἔρως, is the first intimation of the divinities in 'Babette's feast'.

Their second intimation is to be found in Babette's backstory. After Loewenhielm had left the village (never having found a way to communicate his love to Martine), a famous French opera singer, Achille Papin, arrived in the village seeking the spiritual solace of a simple place. Papin soon discovered that Philippa had a marvellous voice, and gained her father's permission to give her singing lessons. One day, he sang a duet from *Don Giovanni* with her and, empassioned by the beauty of their art, 'swept off his feet by the heavenly music and the heavenly voices', he 'drew her toward him and kissed her solemnly, as a bridegroom might kiss his bride before the altar'.[57] For him, there is nothing untoward in this; later, he cannot even remember whether he had kissed her or not: the kiss, to him, was nothing in itself; it was only the pathway to the divine. But for Philippa, this experience of the divine conflicted with her beliefs about her god – showing how the god, in his *essence*, his fixedness of form, can steer us *away* from the holy as easily as towards it – and she reacted to it by asking her father to send Papin away. Fifteen years later, Babette arrives, and presents the sisters with a letter of introduction from Papin. In the letter, he writes to Philippa:

> I feel that you may have chosen the better part in life. What is fame? What is glory? The grave awaits us all! And yet, my lost Zerlina, and yet, soprano of the snow! As I write this I feel that the grave is not the end. In Paradise I shall hear your voice again. There you will sing, without fears or scruples, as God meant you to sing. There you will be the great artist that God meant you to be. Ah! how you will delight the angels.[58]

Papin's thinking about the divine is still cloaked in the fixed forms of religious dogma, but this is, for the most part (though not entirely), inessential. Papin is, now, dwelling in his mortality, and so he is ready to receive the divine, beckoned to it still by Philippa's voice.

That the villagers no longer attend to the holy in the form of the god who appears to them in his essence – indeed, that the villagers' merely formal worship of their god has allowed their attention to drift dismally away from the divine and to become caught up in petty squabbles – is a running theme in 'Babette's feast', and it is essential to the miracle that takes place in the feast. Loewenhielm, who is described as being fashionably pious upon his return to society from the village, and, by the time of the feast, an upright man, more generous of heart by then than the villagers had become, also feels in himself this same kind of drift, though only vaguely: he feels that he is missing something, but does not quite know what it is. The villagers, as well as Loewenhielm, need new divinities to call them back to divinity itself; then, perhaps, the holy will be able to manifest itself once more in their worship of their god.

This is what the feast will provide them with, despite their resistance to it. Having been warned by the sisters that Babette is likely preparing a witch's sabbath for them, the villagers resolve, 'We will cleanse our tongues of all taste and purify them of all delight or disgust of the senses, keeping and preserving them for the higher things of praise and thanksgiving.'[59] They resolve, in other words, to focus their attention solely on the formal commands of their god; they will pay no attention to anything that could draw their attention to divinity – because, as the *Symposium* tells us in its way and Heidegger tells us again in his, only through the senses, only through our bodily nature and not by renouncing it, can we be drawn to divinity. Even the villagers' god allows them a glimpse of this truth. When the feast is about to begin, the villagers think to themselves: 'They were sitting down to a meal, well, so had people done at the wedding of Cana. And grace has chosen to manifest itself there, in the very wine, as fully as anywhere.'[60] In this way they rationalize to themselves their partaking in what they still regard as a sinful affair, but this is what is about to happen to them, despite their resolve that it should not: grace will reveal itself in the very food and wine, as fully as it could anywhere.

Wine is Heidegger's example in 'The thing' of something that draws mortals to the holy – of something through which divinity manifests itself, which is to say, it is his example of a divinity. Wine, on one hand, 'is drink for mortals. It quenches their thirst. It enlivens their conviviality'.[61] The word

Heidegger uses for 'drink' here is not the usual *Getränk* but *Trunk*: a word notable for its association with *betrunkenheit*, drunkenness. On the other hand, he continues, wine

> is at times also given for consecration. If the pouring is for consecration, then it does not still a thirst. It stills the celebration of the feast into the high. The gift of the pouring now is neither given in a tavern nor is the poured gift a drink for mortals. The outpouring is the drink poured out for the immortal gods.

Hofstadter's translation of the last sentence has 'libation' instead of drink, but the word Heidegger uses is *Trank* – still not the usual *Getränk* for drink, but an ordinary enough word, certainly not confined to the strict sense of 'libation' as a drink poured out onto the ground and dedicated to the gods. What Heidegger suggests by using *Trunk* for wine when it is merely drunk by mortals and *Trank* for wine when it is given over to the gods is that the wine merely drunk by mortals is only attended to by them in the way it affects them bodily – wine makes them drunk, as water quenches their thirst – while wine given over to the gods is 'the authentic gift',[62] *if* the gods to whom it is given over are gods in whose form divinity can manifest itself to the wine-drinkers, in that it is wine which gives *mortals* over to divinity. This difference is shown to us in 'Babette's feast', when, all having eaten and drunk together for a while, Loewenhielm rises to speak, and, in speaking, to show not only the meaning of the feast but also that the meaning of the feast is the forgotten meaning of their community. When he rises to speak, 'the old people', who expect nothing so exalted from him but who are already in an exalted state themselves,

> lifted their eyes to the face above them in high, happy expectation. They were used to seeing sailors and vagabonds dead drunk with the crass gin of the country, but they did not recognize in a warrior and courtier the intoxication brought about by the noblest wine of the world.[63]

When the feast is finished, the villagers stumble off into the snowy night; they dance, they fall to the ground, and they laugh. They *are* drunk, but they *are* also elevated, given over to divinity as they have not been for many years:

> It was, to each of them, blissful to have become as a small child; it was also a blessed joke to watch old Brothers and Sisters, who had been

taking themselves so seriously, in this kind of celestial second childhood. They stumbled and got up, walked on or stood still, bodily as well as spiritually hand in hand.[64]

In this description, the narrator makes two gentle corrections to the way those present at Babette's feast understand their experience. The first involves the former seriousness of the villagers having fallen away. The story goes that, 'later in life', the villagers looked back on the night of the feast, they thought that 'the vain illusions of this earth had dissolved before their eyes like smoke, and they had seen the universe as it really is'.[65] There is truth in this thought – it is, indeed, vain illusion; what prevents mortals from dwelling in their mortality and finding their place in the gathered four is the illusion that they are subjects *of* being, responsible for making being happen, rather than subject *to* its happening, that their mastery of things and other people will not end, after all, in the grave – but the villagers' formal religiosity may still prevent it from fully revealing itself: even in the midst of the feast, they interpreted their elevated state as a revelation that 'it was . . . when man has not only altogether forgotten but has firmly renounced all ideas of food and drink that he eats and drinks in the right spirit'.[66]

The second gentle correction in the description of the old villagers dancing in the snow is related to that interpretation; it concerns Loewenhielm's parting words to Martine: 'Every evening I shall sit down, if not in the flesh, which means nothing, in spirit, which is all, to dine with you, just like tonight'.[67] The most profound lesson of the feast, after all, is that the flesh does not mean nothing, and that, on the contrary, the spirit means nothing, there *is* no spirit, without the flesh by way of which *the divinity* beckons us to *divinity*, the holy, the godhead, the happening-to-us of being. This wisdom, if no other, is shared by Galliffet, the ambiguous villain of the story who is remembered by Loewenhielm to have appreciated the ability of a chef at a restaurant in Paris to 'turn a dinner . . . into a kind of love affair – into a love affair of the noble and romantic category in which one no longer distinguishes between bodily and spiritual appetite or satiety!'[68]

The sisters stand outside their house while the villagers dance in the snow, and they look at the sky. ' "The stars have come nearer," said Philippa'.[69] The heavens draw nearer: no mere metaphor. Nearness is the subject with which Heidegger introduces 'The thing', the subject which leads him to describe the thing in terms of the gathered four. Nothing, today, Heidegger begins by saying, is near.[70] Nor is anything distant – 'all distances in space and time are shrinking',[71] yet 'as a result of the abolition of great distances, everything is equally far and equally near . . . as it were, without distance'.[72] Nothing is near because we fail to give ourselves over to things, to their presencing, their drawing near to us. We give ourselves over to things when we hear the message of the beckoning divinities.

At the end of Heidegger's dialogue 'Conversation on a country path about thinking', the three interlocutors say that their walk has 'guided [them] deep into the night . . . that gleams ever more splendidly . . . and overwhelms the stars . . . because it nears their distance in the heavens'.[73] 'Overwhelms' here translates *überstaunen*, a coinage of Heidegger's combining *erstaunen*, to astonish, and *über*, which means *across* as well as over. One might not know how to interpret this if one did not have the *experience* in view that Martine and Philippa have, when, having heard the message of the beckoning divinities, they look at the stars in the sky and see them as having drawn nearer – an experience which I have had walking on a country road at night, afforded the rare space to be a mortal, subject to rather than subject of being. The stars do seem closer, they are brought near: they are not *overwhelmed by* the night, but rather the night *comes astonishingly across* the stars. Elsewhere, Heidegger puts the point more abstractly: 'being transits [*geht über*, goes over/across] (that), comes unconcealingly over (that) which arrives as something of itself unconcealed only by that coming-over [*Überkommnis*]'.[74] What comes across to us through the stars is their being; when we have been beckoned to pay attention to their being, when we are ready to receive their being as the astonishing mystery that it is, then the stars become near to us.

The innocent matter-of-factness of the villagers is what allows them to be so easily exalted. Loewenhielm, on the other hand, is not so innocent; he alone knows, though it seems impossible to him, what is going on in the feast, and so he wonders at it. It seems a strange feature of the story that Loewenhielm's wondering-at is not transformed into wondering-what – he does not go to the kitchen, or even inquire about the chef. But he accepts that the true wonder of the feast is not a wonder that can be answered. This wonder is the unanswerable wonder at the divine mystery of being. That he wonders, and that his wonder is the wonder of a mortal before divinity, is what allows him to respond to the call of being to which all have been beckoned in the feast.

Voice of Fire

Our reception of visual artworks tends to be extremely cognitively loaded. This fact is paradoxical in relation to my purposes here, since one of the

goals of my exploration of my experience with Barnett Newman's painting *Voice of Fire* is to find a way past the cognitive loading of our experience
in general. Indeed, it is commonly believed that art operates by appealing to our emotions rather than by making cognitive-rational claims.
However, when we are 'serious' about artworks, we usually approach
them with the eidetic goal of *knowing* things about them (recalling the
link, which Heidegger emphasizes, in Greek between εἶδος and sight, as
well as Aristotle's musing at the beginning of the *Metaphysics* that human
beings prefer sight to the other senses because it is best for gaining knowledge), of acquiring propositional beliefs about or from them. We want to
know what is 'going on' in the painting, what the artist is 'trying to do',
what techniques are employed. That is, we are concerned with the 'what-
being' of the artwork – and when we are concerned with the 'what-being'
of something, its being itself necessarily remains in the background,
forgotten.

There is a view of art, perhaps the dominant one in our culture, in which
the history of art is conceived as a long conceptual game. Just as philosophy is often conceived as a series of propositional thrusts and parries, with
the history of philosophy moving along as new arguments are invented to
counter, out-do and make irrelevant old ones, art is conceived as a series of
self-referential 'statements' about what art can and should do, with the history of art moving along as new ideas show the limitations of old ones. One
of the main ways in which we are thought to 'appreciate' art is through
indentifying the moves that an artwork makes in this game.

When the history of art is conceived as a conceptual game, all art is
viewed as 'conceptual' art. A work is 'appreciated' when one knows 'what
the artist was trying to do'. A work is admired if the artist is judged to
have been particularly proficient in achieving the conceptual goal. But
our sensuous engagement with the work is occluded. Whenever we ignore
our sensuous engagement with things, treating them merely abstractly, it
is almost impossible for us not to be oblivious of their being. Knowledge
of a thing is one of the ways that the thing's being can happen to us, but
when our relationship with something is purely cognitive, we can imagine
that the way we relate to it is no different from the way an artificial intelligence machines might relate to it. That is, we, like artificial intelligence
machines, simply gather and process data.

We might suppose that an abstract work such as the *Voice of Fire*[75] provides an opportunity for a less cognitively loaded reception of art than
representational works do. Since there are no things depicted in the
Voice of Fire, there is no question of our seeking the cognitive grasp of

'what is in the painting' which tends to dominate our reception of representational works.[76] But this in itself does not guarantee that we will avoid the danger of cognitively overloading our reception of the painting. We do not relate cognitively only to what is 'in' artworks; we also relate cognitively to the works themselves, *as* works of art. This is true not only of academics, who tend to approach artworks from the perspective of some 'theory'; it is also true of members of the gallery-going public, who often approach artworks from the perspective of their knowledge of art history and technique, and even of members of the wider public, who usually have firm ideas about what art ought to be like.

Before I actually saw the *Voice of Fire*, the impression I had gotten of it from photographs and descriptions was that it was basically a piece of conceptual art in this sense. My impression was of something sterile and detached, a 'statement' not only against representationalism but also, with its straight lines and lack of visible brushstrokes or other evidence of the physical contact between painter and painting, against all traces of humanity in art. My impression was that the painting did not need to be experienced because there was nothing in the experience exceeding the ideas it was created to express.

The first time I saw the *Voice of Fire* I had gone to the National Gallery of Canada in Ottawa specifically to see a different painting, namely, Mark Rothko's *#16*. I had recently begun to develop an appreciation for abstract expressionist painting, and I was excited by what I had come to understand about the ideas behind Rothko's paintings. So far, however, I had only seen posters of his work, and I knew that the scale of the works was of their essence; the posters gave me an idea, but the idea (in the case of painting like Rothko's) was not the thing itself. So I went to Ottawa to see *#16*. But when I got to the room in which the abstract expressionists are exhibited, I was immediately and overwhelmingly struck – shocked, in fact – by the *Voice of Fire*. It is that experience I wish to describe.

The *Voice of Fire* is about 18 feet tall and 8 feet wide – in other words, it is an extraordinarily large painting, surprisingly large. It could be described either as consisting of three vertical stripes, one red between two blue, of apparently equal width, or – as it seems more usually described – as consisting of one red stripe on a blue background. No doubt the latter description tends to be preferred because the red dominates one's experience of the painting. The red – which verges slightly on orange – and the blue are both very vivid, and both appear more or less completely homogeneous in shade and texture; the borders between the red and blue are, for all intents and purposes, perfectly straight.

I have said that, when I first saw the *Voice of Fire*, I was *shocked* by it. What shocked me was its simple, insistent *presence*, a presence that insistingly presents itself right across the room and out of the door. The room is laid out so as to maximize the sense of its presence; the *Voice of Fire* is framed by the main entrance to the room so that, if one is not distracted and one's attention is directed into the room as one approaches, the *Voice of Fire* will dominate one's experience of the room before one even enters. But it is no accident that the room is designed this way – it does not create the insistent presence of the *Voice of Fire*; it accommodates and allows for it. Rothko's *#16* (as I discovered, to my disappointment, on that initial trip), for instance, could not have the same insistent presence even if it occupied the place of the *Voice of Fire*.

Now I will attempt to describe the shocking experience of the insistent presence of the *Voice of Fire*. The first thing to note is that in that experience, other things became less relevant. This includes other things that had weighed on my attention before I entered the room and would weigh on my attention after I left the room, and also other things in the room. But, like the things I had left behind and would encounter later outside the room, the other things in the room were other than the *Voice of Fire* in a temporal as well as a spatial sense. Moving around a gallery, my attention is almost always divided between the work I am looking at in the present, the things I have been doing in the more or less recent past – including, but not only, looking at other works – and (especially) the things I might be doing in the more or less near future – predominantly including looking at other works I want to look at (perhaps in the same room, perhaps already in my peripheral vision), and leaving the gallery, which, together, affect my experience of the work I am looking at presently in that they make me aware of the need to limit the time I spend with it. If I had been subject to that effect when I saw the *Voice of Fire*, then my experience of it would have been affected by the future possibility of viewing the other works in the room. But this was not the case, for that short time – likely half an hour at most – when I first encountered the painting. For that time, my attention was *fixed* on that one thing. There was, we may say, an extraordinarily tight *fitting-together* between the painting and me, a fitting-together free of interference from other claims on my attention. In that fitting-together the being of the painting impressed itself on me, into me. Let there be no mistake here: what impressed itself on me was the *being* of the painting, but it was not, so to speak, the being *of the painting*, as this expression would be understood metaphysically. The connection between the painting and me did not consist in, or even allow for, the transmission of an 'essence' (in the metaphysical sense) from the painting to me. I gained no *knowledge* from or about the painting in this experience (except, of course, that the painting was particularly able to allow such an experience to take place, but this is not something I was thinking of at the time).

The division – which we might call the 'temporal dispersion' – of attention that I have described in relation to viewing artworks is something that happens almost all the time, almost everywhere, in my experience of almost everything. This is related to what Heidegger calls the 'ecstatic' nature of the temporality of human existence, our being 'stretched' between past and future. When I enter the gallery, I carry with me my whole past, but likely what I currently experience of that past is only what has left a particularly strong impression on me – perhaps I am flustered, still dwelling in the experience of not knowing where I was going on the way here, or perhaps I am agitated and hostile, still dwelling in the experience of an entirely unrelated disagreement I had with someone earlier in the day – or what is particularly pertinent to my current situation – perhaps I am annoyed with myself for arriving later than I would have liked, my attention still drawn back to the unimportant things I could have skipped doing to get here sooner. Entering the gallery I also carry with me the whole of my future possibilities, but again, those that are part of my current experience are only those that seem particularly pertinent to me – there are certain things that I want to see, the gallery closes at a certain time, I might get hungry, I hope it isn't too cold when I leave.

The temporal range of my current experience constantly varies, ranging over sometimes more, sometimes less of my past and future. Sometimes it is focused almost completely on the past; other times, almost completely on the future. Sometimes it is particularly focused on the present – as, for instance, it is while I am writing these words, though possible futures, in which I will revise what I have written, and in which others will read it, are always near to the focus of my experience. The inability to maintain the focus of one's experience in the present often results in unhappiness, relative both to deep happiness and to happiness as it is more commonly understood. For instance, the mood of *anxiety* (which, again, we must distinguish from *Angst* as a Heideggerian way of being attuned) comes over us when we struggle to shift the focus of our attention from future possibilities to the things that we want to devote our attention to in the present. I interrupt my writing to read the newspaper – an easier, more immediately pleasurable activity. But the future possibilities of writing, and especially the future possibilities of failing to have written what I need to have written by this or that time for this or that purpose, still tug at me insistently.

Though reading the newspaper is pleasurable, I am not happy doing it, I am uneasy, *unheimlich*, unable to focus – I do not dwell in my fitting-together with the newspaper (for there is a kind of fitting-together even in the sheer cognitive transfer of information), and because of that I do not fit in my present situation, but rather part of me, part of my experience of my receptivity to being, is outside my present situation, pulling on me.

Similarly, a mood of what we might call depression or melancholy can result from the same kind of tension between past and present: the weight of the past, particularly of past failures, can take the focus of one's experience out of the present, causing one to slow to a stop in the present. Taking again the example of my writing here, it is difficult to write when my experience dwells in parts that have not gone well, or when it dwells in all the time that has gone by in which I have accomplished little. The focus of my experience in the past pulls on me in the present, pulls me away from what I am trying to focus on in the present – again, interfering with the *fit* between me and what I am trying to engage with in the present, preventing me from dwelling in it.

These examples show that the 'temporal dispersion' of experience can be a source of unhappiness. If this is so, then it follows that overcoming the temporal dispersion of experience at least contributes to happiness. We might note that when our experience is focused in the present, alternatives to our current situation are not available to our experience (since all alternatives lie in the future), and thus we cannot want our situation to be different (at least, in any *particular* way) – and this has traditionally been thought to be one of the main characteristics of happiness. However, that we do not want our situation to be any different is not sufficient to show that we are happy; we could just be resigned. The fact that the temporal dispersion of experience can be a source of unhappiness does not entail that we will become happy just by overcoming this dispersion, and, in fact, that is not all it takes to be happy. For instance, when we watch television, play video games or engage in other 'mindless' activities (including, frequently, reading the newspaper), our experience is often very much focused in the present, so much so that, having lost contact with past and future, we 'lose track of the time' – but it often strains most ordinary senses of 'happiness' beyond the breaking point to call ourselves 'happy' at these times. Indeed, we can be deeply unhappy when our experience is strictly focused in the present; this is the case, for example, when our attention is consumed by physical discomfort.

The insistent presence of the *Voice of Fire*, the insistence of the happening-to-me of its being, induced me to set everything else aside to take it in, to set aside everything I might have thought about it and have been prepared to do in relation to it, and simply let it be to me. My attitude towards it became one that might be described in part as an attitude of 'reverence'. The apprehension *that the painting is* (which is also an apprehension that *Es gibt Sein* in general) is an apprehension that the being of the painting (and being in general) is worthy of reverence. But this is not a cognitive apprehension that, as a matter of fact, being *should* be revered, with the result that one directs oneself to revere being; it cannot be that, because in such a cognitive judgement *about* a thing's being, it would be treated as an object, and a distance would be opened up between oneself and the being of a thing – the *fitting-together* between oneself and the being of the thing, in which its being is fulfilled, would be disrupted. Rather, in the apprehension of a thing's being, being *is* revered. Indeed, the etymology of the word 'reverence' reveals the association between reverence and the apprehension of being: 'reverence' is traced to the Proto-Indo-European root *wer-*, meaning 'to be or become aware of'.[77] To revere something is to become aware of it, in a special sense: to revere something is to be deeply *affected* by awareness of it. The immediate etymological antecedent of 'reverence' is the Latin *reverentia*, the root of which is *vereri*, meaning 'to stand in awe of' or 'to fear'. To fear something is one way of being affected by awareness of it, but of course our sense of 'reverence' tends to present other, more positive ways of being affected by awareness of things.

Reverence is founded on mystery, and to revere something is to consider it holy; the happening-to-us of being is the greatest mystery of all, more holy than any being could be. If we subordinated being's holiness to that of a god by attributing the creation of being's happening-to-us to a god, we would fail to capture the depth of its holiness: as Heidegger says, interpreting Hölderlin, any god 'still remains beneath [the holy]'.[78] Whatever god there may be does not create the holy, the mysterious *lighting up* of beings that is their being, but 'takes upon himself that which is "above" him, the holy, and brings it together into the sharpness and force of the unique ray through which he is "allotted" to man, in order to bestow it'. Of course, Heidegger does not have in mind a creator god, but that case is no different: a god could create that which is, but there seems no way to make sense of the idea that a god could make that which is *be*, in the full sense of being that Heidegger has pointed us towards. The god can make beings such that they have the capacity to be to us, and the god can create us such that we have the capacity to receive the being of that which is – but being itself, that which happens in the *Ereignis* of our fitting together with the being of beings, is not something that a being such as a god could create.[79]

As we saw in the Introduction, one of the ways in which we might classify happiness is as an *affect*. Affects *affect* us, they come over us – they are the way that our engagement with the world 'feels' to us. I have indicated that I was *affected* by the *Voice of Fire* in saying that I said that I was *shocked* by it. We might ordinarily think of 'shock' as a 'feeling' in its own right – for instance, when we are shocked, we inhale sharply, our hearts pound, our eyes widen. These are the physiological effects of shock in a familiar form, namely, sudden fright. But what is characteristic of 'shock' is that it is a sudden wrenching from one affective state into another, not necessarily into fright in particular. It seems likely the case that when we speak of shock, the affective state into which we are wrenched is usually a 'negative' one – for instance, when we speak of 'shocking news', it is generally sad news, news that wrenches us into a state of sadness – but this is not always the case. It does not strain the word to say that we are 'shocked with joy', that is, shocked into joy; if, without warning, I were reunited with a loved one I had given up for dead, I would certainly be shocked – I would be wrenched into a state of joy.

In the experience of the *Voice of Fire*, I was wrenched into a state of deep happiness. What, finally, can I say to describe this state? So far I have said that it involved a focus on the present that forecloses the anxiety resulting from the tension between present and future focuses of experience (and the 'depression' resulting from a similar tension between present (and future) and past). I have also said that it involved *reverence*. But what, we want to know, did it *feel* like? Perhaps we even want to ask: all that aside, did it feel *happy*? The urge to ask this question may be motivated by the assumption that happiness is the kind of 'simple, unanalyzable property' that G. E. Moore claimed goodness to be, and that Moore's 'open question argument' about goodness – that is, that any putative analysis of goodness in terms of some quality will fail to close the question whether something with that quality is actually good or not – applies to happiness as well.[80] Or, if our prejudices are more hedonistic, we might want to ask: but did it feel *pleasant*?

If, in the end, all we are left with is these questions, then we have gotten nowhere. The best I could do in answer to the question 'But what did it *feel* like?' is to answer in terms of my bodily response to the *Voice of Fire*: I became limp, relaxed, pliable, loose – in other words, open and receptive to its being, no longer in the more or less tense posture of challenge or defence that characterizes my bodily comportment most of the time. The restless bodily urge to move along vanished; my body seemed to both deflate and expand, settling into and filling out its location in the middle of the room. These descriptions map onto what I have said about the experience already, in fairly obvious ways. When my experience of my situation is anxiously focused on future possibilities, my body is tense, hardening itself against uncertain threats; tense muscles clench, tire and ache, so that anxiety is literally *felt* as physical discomfort. But more importantly, the way that moods such as anxiety and depression engage us with things typically has to do with our attitude towards those things as the kind of things they are, which means that those moods have to do with some kind of readiness (or unreadiness) for action in relation to things. Deep happiness brings with it a 'feeling' of relaxation because the mood of deep happiness does not relate us to things as things to be dealt with, as calling for action; it relates us to the being of things.

These descriptions of the bodily 'feelings' associated with happiness in our sense do not exactly tell us 'how happiness feels' – we can be relaxed and peaceful in a state of stupor as well as in a state of happiness. These bodily feelings are not, then, sufficient for or even unique to deep happiness, but they do seem to be necessary to deep happiness. The descriptions of bodily 'feelings', like all the other descriptions in this section, do not tell us *what* deep happiness *is*, but rather help us to identify *where* it *might happen* – they tell us where to look for deep happiness. No doubt this may seem unsatisfying, but recall what I said in Chapter 2: because deep happiness, like being itself, is not a *thing*, we will not be able to say *what it is* (although it helps us to get a sense of deep happiness if we describe it as a mood, just as it helps us to a sense of being if we describe it as a happening). Thus what we are aiming to do is not to say what happiness or being is, but to recover the *experience* of being from its oblivion – not to say *what* that experience is, but to help us to remember *that* we do experience being – and to show that the experience of being, the experience in which we dwell in our fitting-together with being, is the experience in which deep happiness consists.

Fitting Together with the Being of Others

Heidegger is often taken to task for (and sometimes credited with) being an extreme individualist. This criticism is usually directed at *Being and Time*, with its exhortations to 'win' oneself back from one's 'lostness' in 'the they'. As the interpretation of Heidegger underlying this criticism has it, other human beings can only interrupt the solitary thinker's relationship with being. But of course other human beings *are*, too, and there is no reason that we cannot think being by engaging with the being of other human beings. In fact, it is in our relationships with other human beings that most of us engage with being most intensely. Nearly everyone at least understands and desires intimate contact with other human beings. And our desire for intimate contact is not just a physiologically instinctive drive for *physical* contact. *Purely* physical contact, as in the contact between two inanimate objects, is not at all the sort of contact we desire to have with other human beings – indeed, as long as we are conscious, we are not even capable of that kind of contact. The being of every thing that comes into physical contact with us engages with our receptivity to being, and thus *affects* us. What we desire from contact with other human beings is reciprocal *affection*, in a literal sense; that is, we desire to be affected by their being, and we desire that they will be affected by ours.

Intimate engagement with the being of another human being is an important if not defining feature of love. Of course, it is not my intention to define 'love' or propose a theory of love here, though I would suggest that love is part of the same constellation of fittingness as being and happiness. In other words, I would suggest that it is no accident that love and happiness go together, in the same way that, for Plato, it is no accident that justice and happiness go together. To the extent that we succeed in relating to others, to the extent that we experience, dwell in and affirm the fitting-together of their being and our capacity to receive it – to that extent, we love them.

Love, in this sense, is not (as it is sometimes thought to be) an altogether different phenomenon from being 'in love' – in fact, in what follows I will describe the experience of being in love as a particularly intense *form* of love, which prepares the way for the longer-term love that follows between intimate partners. The 'thrill' of being 'in love' should not be confused with 'infatuation', insofar as 'infatuation' not only lacks reciprocation but also characteristically has merely some idea, some representation, of another person as its object. What *is* the 'thrill' of being 'in love' – this feeling which may be the most universally acknowledged and sought after occasion for happiness in our culture? We are familiar with *explanations*, psychological and physiological, of why we fall in love, of what the purpose of falling in love is, either for the continuation of the species or for our own self-esteem and self-actualization. But what *is* the phenomenon of 'being in love' itself? The answer I will suggest to this question will also suggest at least a partial answer to the question why we typically cannot be in love continuously with one person indefinitely, though it may happen indefinitely that, from time to time, the feeling returns of being in love with someone, whom one was once in love with and still loves. It will also suggest a partial answer to the question why our most abiding love is often for children.

The last extended time of great happiness in my life was the time of being in love with my partner. One of the things that characterized that time of being in love was that it was a time of revelation. At first, my partner and I were almost completely unknown to each other; in a matter of weeks, I learned almost everything about her, and she about me. We were far more open towards each other than human beings ordinarily are either towards each other or towards other things. Absent from our way of relating to each other was the distance people normally maintain between each other due to their experience of their relationships being dominated by their cognitive way of relating to each other. Ordinarily, when we encounter other people, we regard them as objects about which information is to be acquired and processed. And this is our attitude towards others most of the time even in our most intimate relationships – which, after all, involve mostly the negotiation of the mundane activities of everyday life – as evidenced by the vast popular literature purporting to help people acquire, interpret, and respond to information about their partners.

Recall the discussion above concerning the cognitively loaded way in which we ordinarily experience visual artworks, and how that was overcome in the experience with the *Voice of Fire*: something very similar happened in my experience of being in love. But it seems as if there is a contradiction here: if my experience of being in love was characterized by revelation and learning, how could it be that my engagement with my partner was not cognitively loaded in the way that our experience of other human beings ordinarily is? Recall the description of my experience with the language of 'The tuft of flowers': there, I said that what was at stake was not a matter of *knowing* anything, but that does not mean that there was no cognitive element to the experience. The cognitive is one of being's ways of happening to us: things present themselves to us cognitively, among other ways. While I could know (in the usual, if incomplete, senses) what the language of the poem sought to tell me without having the sort of experience which makes that knowledge meaningful, I could not have had that experience without gaining the knowledge. Similarly, the experience of being in love involved a cognitive engagement – it involved the acquisition of knowledge – but what made it an experience of being in love was that *through* the knowledge I acquired about my partner I was engaged with her being. She *was*, her being *happened to me*, in part through the knowledge that I gained of her. Thus when I would tell my close friends what I had learned about her, I would be almost as happy as I was when I was with her: in bringing my knowledge of her to language, I would be engaged once again with her being.

So, perhaps, here is one reason (though others seem obvious) why we ordinarily cannot be in love with the same person indefinitely: after the initial, intense period of revelation, there is not so much left for us to learn about the other person. And this, too, could be one reason why our most abiding love is often for children: because children are constantly developing new ways of being, there is no end to the revelation that is possible in our relationships with them. (Likewise, children are always developing new ways in which they are receptive to the being of their close family members, as well as everything else, and what close family members are willing and able to reveal of themselves to children changes as children grow up.) However, we never finally come to the end of what we can learn about our intimate adult partners, either. This is necessarily so because all human beings, as long as their capacities are not too diminished, are always at least capable of developing new ways of being.

Of course, one of the great sources of anxiety in intimate relationships is the possibility that our partners will change, or may already have changed, in ways which will close off the connections between us. This points to something that may seem to have been overlooked so far: we do not fall in love with just anyone, with people who *are* just any*how*. My description of being in love may seem to run the risk of eliding this fact, and indeed it may seem to encourage an elision of the particularity of the other person which could be practically dangerous as well as theoretically suspect. Being in love is a dwelling in our fitting-together with the being of another person, in the same way that my experience with the *Voice of Fire* was a dwelling in my fitting-together with the being of the painting. The *being* with which we fit together is not the essence (in the metaphysical sense) of the particular thing but the *happening to us* which everything that is has in common. Thus the reverence for the being of the *Voice of Fire* was described as a reverence before being per se. However, not all paintings are equally capable of occasioning the kind of experience I had with the *Voice of Fire*. In fact, *only* the *Voice of Fire*, among visual artworks, has occasioned such a powerful experience of fitting-together with being for me, and it is its particular way of being that made it able to do so – and so I love that painting in a way that I do not love any other. Similarly, only my partner has occasioned for me such a powerful experience of fitting-together with the being of another human being, and it was the particular way in which she is that led me to open myself to the revelation of her being – and so I love her in a way that I do not love any other.

Experiences of what we ordinarily speak of as love – the love between intimate partners or between close family members – are not, of course, the only experiences in which we dwell in our fitting-together with the being of other human beings, though they are generally the most intense. That is to say, they are generally the *happiest* experiences occasioned by the being of other human beings. But we can be perhaps equally happy when, for instance, we are engaged in intense and invigorating conversation. Often such conversation is a manifestation of the love belonging to an ongoing relationship of friendship, but it does not have to be – indeed, it can happen with people whom we have never encountered before and will never engage with again. We can even have experiences of happiness in fitting together with the being of another human being without ever meeting or having any kind of direct exchange with that person. This can happen, for instance, when we read things that other people have written. I had such an experience in reading the first page of Nabokov's *Pale Fire*, as the being of *Nabokov* struck me, standing out in his singular style, through the startling sentence in which the narrator notes, relevant to nothing he is saying but revealing much about his saying of it, that 'there is a very loud amusement park right in front of my present lodgings'.[81]

I will conclude by briefly describing another experience of happiness I once had in fitting together with the being of someone whom I not only never met or exchanged words with, but who was completely anonymous to me (as the mower was to Frost's narrator). I was sitting in a small piano practice room in a university music building; from another room, I could hear someone playing a piece I was familiar with, Chopin's 'Revolutionary Étude'. The pianist played it well, but not perfectly, so that the *person* playing was very evident in the music. I could *hear* both the pianist's happiness in the engagement with the music when it was going well, and the pianist's anxious struggle to regain that engagement when it began to break down. Fitting together with the pianist's being, I was *affected* by the pianist's struggle. I was 'gripped' by the music, because the music presented the pianist to me: the pianist *was* in and through the music; the music *fit together* my receptivity to being with the pianist's being, and I sat alone (but 'no more alone'!) and still in my small room, dwelling in my fitting-together with the being of the pianist.

Chapter 4

The History of Being

Overview of Heidegger's History of Being

Heidegger says that 'we are bound to the characterization of being as presencing [*Anwesenheit*]', because 'this character of being has long since been decided'.[1] I sometimes speak of the happening-to-us of being in the sense of *Ereignis* as a 'presencing', but the German *Anwesenheit* has a sense built into it that the English 'presencing' does not, which inclines *Anwesenheit* (and indeed also 'presencing' in its Latin roots,[2] though the roots are much more obscure in the English word than in the German) towards being in the sense of its epochal destinings. Embedded in *Anwesenheit* is the root *Wesen*, the word for 'essence' that was discussed in the previous chapter. *An-wesen-heit* is literally 'essencing-to-ness': it is the happening of something's coming to us in its essence, the happening of something's essence taking shape in its approach to and encounter with us. Thus *Anwesenheit*, for Heidegger, is bound up with the history of being and its historical reception as metaphysical philosophy.

The lecture – 'Time and being' – in which Heidegger says that it has long been decided that being is *Anwesenheit* is the place in which Heidegger suggests a version of the 'destruction' or 'dismantling' (*Destruktion*) of the history of metaphysics that was projected for the never-published Part Two of *Being and Time*.[3] But the lecture takes place in 1962, long after the 'turn' in Heidegger's thinking. The destruction of the history of metaphysics now means the analysis of the history of being as it is destined to us in its epochs. In *Being and Time*, Heidegger's project was to clear away the successive metaphysical interpretations of being that had obscured the temporal happening of being. In 'Time and being', Heidegger's view is that once we see that metaphysical philosophy has always been concerned with the epochal ways in which being has been sent to us, we can turn our attention to what most needs to be thought, namely, the sending itself, the happening-to-us of being, *Ereignis*.

As we saw in the Introduction, Heidegger links his word 'epoch' to the Greek ἐποχή, emphasizing that every epoch of being is not only a way that being presences but also a way that being is 'held back' – *An sich halten* as well as *An-wesen-heit*.[4] We can identify three senses of holding-back. First, each epoch holds back other epochal ways of presencing. Second, each epoch holds back the fact that it is an epochal way of presencing. Third, each epoch holds back the fact of the presencing, the sending, the happening-to-us of being itself. The second sense is relatively straightforward: as long as we are under the sway of a given epochal way of presencing, we understand being in its way; we need to be outside it in order to recognize it as one epochal way of presencing among others. The first and third senses of holding-back are more complicated.

In order to understand them, we should first note that Heidegger never tells the story of the history of being completely and definitively. A basic sketch would run from the φύσις of the pre-Socratics to the ἰδέαι of Plato to the God-created world of the medievals to the calculable objects of the moderns to the human will-full world of the last two centuries, but Heidegger constantly varies this scheme.[5] This can be accounted for partly by the fact that, on his view, 'epoch does not mean . . . a span of time',[6] so there can be no definite chronology of epochs and it might be somewhat misleading to present the history of being in chronological form, although as it happens the epochs he identifies can be identified to greater and lesser degrees with particular historical periods. The epoch of *Ge-Stell*, which I will examine in the next section, is strongly identified with the current historical time. But though *Ge-Stell* dominates our time, it is not the only epoch of being that holds sway. The Platonic doctrine of ἰδέαι is also the thought of an epoch of being, and it holds sway over us whenever we are concerned with what a thing is as the particular kind of thing it is. The way being presences in *Ge-Stell* holds back the way being presences as ἰδέαι, but not to the extent that the latter is no longer available to us.

While in any given period a particular epoch of being is likely to be dominant, 'the epochs overlap [*überdecken*] each other'[7] – and in their overlapping, 'the original sending of being as presence is more and more obscured in different ways'. The latter claim has to do with the third sense of holding-back. It is progressively more difficult to identify each epoch of being as an epoch of being because, as Heidegger lays out most explicitly in the *Nietzsche* lectures,[8] the successive epochs of being make it seem more and more like *we* are the ground of being – in fact, we might say that the history of metaphysics, on Heidegger's view, is the history of a refinement and purification of the notion that we are the ground of being, the traces of which are evident in Protagoras and Plato and which reaches its culmination in Nietzsche's doctrine of the will to power. Being as mutual appropriation is more and more obscured as the sending, the 'in-flashing', fades from view in favour of the receiving, the 'in-sight'.

According to Heidegger, one of the oldest epochs of the history of being, if not the oldest epoch, is that of φύσις[9] (which we commonly translate as 'nature', though this is problematic, as I will discuss below), which Heidegger identifies primarily with the pre-Socratic Greeks. Φύσις, it seems, is the epochal sending of being which least obscures the sending, the happening-to-us, of being itself, *Ereignis*. If we can go back through the epochs to dwell in φύσις, we will find ourselves already very close to dwelling in *Ereignis*. When we are under the sway of the epochal sending of *Ge-Stell*, it is a vast leap to the thought of *Ereignis*, but when we are under the sway of the epochal sending of φύσις, it is only a short jump. That we must make a vast leap to get to the thought of *Ereignis* from within *Ge-Stell* means that we also must make a vast leap to apprehend what makes us deeply happy; it means that we are threatened with complete obliviousness of what makes us deeply happy, such that we will be deeply happy only by accident if at all. From within the epochal sending of φύσις, on the other hand, the apprehension of what makes us deeply happy is only a short jump away. I will try to illustrate this in the final section of this chapter.

Seinsvergessenheit, Ge-Stell and 'The Last Men'

One of the markers of the shift between the earlier and later Heidegger is the appearance of the term *Seinsvergessenheit* (which he spells *Seynsvergessenheit* when he is using the spelling *Seyn*): forgetting or oblivion of being. The notion that being has been forgotten is not altogether new to the later Heidegger. The Introduction to *Being and Time* begins with the statement that the question of being has been forgotten. This *question* has been forgotten by those whose task it might be to question, that is, philosophers: 'it sustained the avid research of Plato and Aristotle but from then on ceased to be heard *as a thematic question of actual investigation*'.[10] With the 'turn' in Heidegger's thinking, however, he begins to claim that not just the *question* of being but *being itself* is forgotten – from which it follows as a matter of course that philosophers do not question concerning being – and *Seinsvergessenheit* becomes one of his guiding words. We can see this shift in the first chapter of *An Introduction to Metaphysics*, which is the text of a lecture course given in 1935, in the midst of the 'turn'. There, Heidegger is still concerned, as in *Being and Time*, to ask the question of the *meaning* of being, and, as at the beginning of *Being and Time*, he explains this project by way of distinguishing between the questioning concerning *beings* characterizing contemporary metaphysics and his own questioning concerning *being* per se.[11] But now he emphasizes that 'the fault' for the failure to question concerning being 'did not begin with us, or with our immediate or more remote ancestors, but lies in something that runs through Western history from the very beginning', namely, that 'we have fallen out [*herausgefallen*] of being'.[12] A note to this passage refers the reader to §38 of *Being and Time*, the section concerning *Verfallenheit*, that is, 'fallenness', 'entanglement', or (as Stambaugh translates it) 'falling prey'. But clearly this does not mean that the same point is being made in both texts. In *Being and Time*, *Verfallenheit* is described as an 'ontological-existential structure' of *Da-Sein*, which therefore has no historical inception and cannot 'be removed in the advanced stages of human culture'.[13] In *An Introduction to Metaphysics*, however, our falling out of being is a historical occurrence, one which Heidegger now wants in some way to overturn.

This becomes clearer in the *Contributions*. There, Heidegger writes that 'forgottenness of being' – *Seynsvergessenheit* – is grounded in 'abandonment of being' – *Seynsverlassenheit*.[14] With the latter concept, Heidegger emphasizes that the 'forgetting of being' is not a failure of human agency. Almost two decades later, in 'On the question of being', Heidegger would put the same point this way:

> We all too readily run the danger of understanding forgottenness merely as a human act or activity. People have . . . tended to represent the 'forgottenness of being' as though, to say it by way of an image, being were the umbrella that has been left sitting somewhere through the forgetfulness of some philosophy professor.[15]

Given how *Being and Time* frames the problem of the forgotten question concerning the meaning of being, it is understandable that people would represent the forgottenness of being that way, since that indeed seems to be the way *Being and Time* itself represents the problem. It is only with Heidegger's new notion of the 'history of being' that *Seynsvergessenheit* can be seen as something underlying the whole history of the Western engagement with being, rather than as something that is the fault of inattentive philosophers.

In the *Contributions*, Heidegger writes that '*abandonment of beings by being* means that being [*Seyn*] has withdrawn from beings'.[16] This withdrawal, says Heidegger, 'is not simply "decline" but the earliest history of being itself, the history of the first beginning'.[17] By 'the first beginning' Heidegger means the beginning of Western thought concerning being, most decisively manifest in Plato and the thought that the being of a thing consists in a certain kind of being, namely, its ἰδέα. If *Seynsvergessenheit* can be said to begin with this particular figure, Plato, then we might wonder why it cannot be said to be merely a matter of a conventional kind of forgetting, why it might not be a matter akin to forgetting one's umbrella – does not Plato *overlook* being itself, *Seyn*, in characterizing the being of a being as something which is itself a being? Why can we not say that we owe *Seynsvergessenheit* to Plato's *negligence*, which the subsequent history of philosophy has, negligently, failed to correct? If Plato had never lived, might the history of Western thought not have developed differently, in a way which did not fail to keep being in view?

We do not seem to have any ground on which to insist that this could not have happened. But the important thing is that the thought of being as ἰδέα is not simply a creation of Plato's, simply his interpretation of being. It is a way that being presents itself. Recall Heidegger's thought of the turning, the reciprocal appropriation between being and human being: in-sight into being and the in-flashing of being are two sides of the same coin; the happening of being is fulfilled in and as our experience of it. Thus, as Heidegger says in 'On the question of being', 'oblivion does not simply *befall* the essence of being, as something apparently separate from the latter. It belongs to the issue of being itself, prevails as a destiny of its essence.'[18] If one devotes oneself to thinking about being, 'listens' to being, asks how beings are present to one, it is not in any way illegitimate or false to respond that beings present themselves essentially as ἰδέαι – the naming of that in-sight into being makes manifest in thought a certain truth, unconcealment, of being. In a particular historical moment it might be the only way, or at least the most fitting way, to respond to the call of being. We may venture that it is indeed the most fitting response at the moment we see reflected in the works of Plato, a moment in which the meanings of important words such as 'virtue', 'justice', 'knowledge' and 'beauty' have come into question and it becomes necessary to look for something that will determine their meaningfulness. As soon as it becomes necessary to look – which is to say, to look through the conflicting guises in which virtue, justice, knowledge and beauty appear – then these things, insofar as they are anything at all, *present themselves* as ἰδέαι.

But why is *Seyn* obscured in this thinking of the being of beings? It is obscured because this thinking is concerned to discover the being of beings in order to help us out of some practical problem. Being is thought as ἰδέα so that we can know what, for instance, justice is, and we want to know what justice is so that we can know what we ought to do. Or, in Heidegger's more concrete example in 'The thing', one calls upon the ἰδέα of a thing in order to bring just such a thing into being, for instance a jug:

> In the process of its making . . . the jug must first show its outward appearance [*Aussehen*] to the maker. But what shows itself here, the outward appearance (the *eidos*, the *idea*), characterizes the jug solely in the respect in which the vessel stands over against the maker as something to be made.[19]

In other words, the thinking of being in the metaphysical tradition is biased from the beginning towards the presentation of being as determined by human needs and desires, by human will. This is why, for Heidegger, Nietzsche represents the culmination of metaphysics. Every previous metaphysical interpretation of the being of beings is shown up by Nietzsche as nothing other than will to power. For Nietzsche, then, the history of metaphysics is the history of nihilism – everything hitherto posited as being is *nothing* but projection of some formation of will to power – and his own philosophy, thinking the thought that all must eventually think, heralds the age when that nihilism is 'consummated' through the realization of the nullity of every purported being. Thus Heidegger writes in 'On the question of being' that 'in the phase of consummate nihilism, it looks as though there were no such thing as the *being* of beings . . . . Being remains absent in a strange way. It conceals itself. It maintains itself in a concealment that conceals itself'.[20]

This brings us back to the statement in the *Contributions* that the oblivion of being is not a 'decline' but goes back to the earliest history of being. However, when, in the late 1940s, Heidegger comes to think what Nietzsche calls the age of consummate nihilism as the epoch of *Ge-Stell*, 'enframement' as the essence of modern technology, he will pronounce this particular sending of being as the greatest danger to the possibility of the recovery of *Seyn*. His most intensive treatment of *Ge-Stell* occurs in a lecture originally called simply '*Das Ge-Stell*', which was later expanded into '*Die Frage nach der Technik*' and translated into English as 'The question concerning technology'. '*Das Ge-Stell*' is the second of a set of four lectures, first given in 1949, which begins with 'The thing' and ends with 'The turning'. (The remaining lecture, '*Die gefahr*', 'The danger', which refers to the danger posed by *Ge-Stell*, was not published in Heidegger's lifetime.) It could be said that *Ge-Stell* is the topic of the lecture series as a whole, and even though it is not named in 'The thing', the opening of 'The thing' implicitly introduces the problem of *Ge-Stell*, by way of a discussion of distance and nearness. The lecture begins with the proposition that 'all distances in space and time are shrinking'.[21] Distance was being shrunk – and how much more so today, it seems – most obviously by the ready access that modern technologies give us to formerly foreign places and events. By now it seems within the power of the average Western urbanite to see anywhere, almost to be anywhere and to become familiar with anything on Earth, instantaneously.

Yet, Heidegger says, 'the frantic abolition of all distances brings no nearness; for nearness does not consist in shortness of distance';[22] indeed, 'as a result of the abolition of great distances, everything is equally far and equally near', or rather, 'everything is neither far nor near – is, as it were, without distance'.[23] Everything is without distance – indeed, every thing fails to *be* a thing, fails to 'thing' – because we fail to be 'gathered' in the thing, in the sense explored in the section on the gathered four in Chapter 3. Nothing is near, because nearness consists in our being gathered, together with divinities, earth and sky, in things: 'nearness is at work in bringing near, as the thinging of the thing'.[24]

The series of lectures is designed to show how the epochal sending of being as *Ge-Stell* threatens the 'thinging' of the thing in a particularly dangerous way. Modern technology allows human beings to live under the assumption that there is no limit to the realization of human will. As a result, everything that is presents itself to us primarily in its potential for the realization of human will. This, for Heidegger, is the real significance of Nietzsche's doctrine of the will to power: it is not the one, final, true interpretation of reality itself, but an acutely attentive response to the sending of being in our epoch. Under the sway of *Ge-Stell*, everything, including ourselves, is presented as actual or potential force; things presented as potential force Heidegger calls *Bestand*, commonly translated as 'standing-reserve'.[25] We are presented to ourselves as nodes of force – in the form of will and of our bodily capacities to realize the wills of ourselves or others – that act on and are acted on by other forces in the general flux. What is of significance in anything or anyone is its potential for acting, for initiating and responding to force, bringing about or realizing some effect.

Hence, in Heidegger's example in 'The question concerning technology', the Rhine is present to us as a 'standing-reserve' of various kinds of forces waiting to be tapped. This is so not only in the obvious sense of the river's being a source of hydro-electric power, but in subtler ways such as its being 'an object on call for inspection by a tour group ordered there by the vacation industry'.[26] And the forces at play in the latter instance are not only, or perhaps even primarily, economic. The Rhine shows up as a standing reserve of forces in the tourists' *aesthetic experience* of it, in its ability to act upon them, to produce an emotional response, to *delight* them or to *move* them.[27] The distance between the tourists and the Rhine is dissolved in the flux of forces that unites them.

One of the main themes in 'The question concerning technology' is the relationship between technology and truth. Heidegger writes: 'What is modern technology? It . . . is a revealing. Only when we allow our attention to rest on this fundamental characteristic does that which is new in modern technology show itself to us'.[28] Both modern and earlier technologies reveal something of earth and sky in making use of them. The difference, according to Heidegger, is that modern technologies 'challenge' earth and sky as earlier ones do not. To illustrate this he contrasts an old windmill with the process of deriving energy from coal. The windmill leaves the surrounding world, including the wind itself, much as it is. This is not to say that the windmill does not impose upon the surrounding world, or that its erection may not be seen, as much as the erection of a modern technological installation, as an act of violence against the surrounding world. The point is that the windmill does not transform the surrounding world into something unrecognizable by rendering it into quanta of force. The wind turns the blades, the blades turn a shaft, the shaft turns the stone that grinds the wheat. The relation between the motion of the wind and the motion of the wheel is immediately apparent. Sky *shows up in* the grinding of the wheat. The *power* of the wind is not removed from it to be used in a way which will allow us to forget about the wind, as anything other than power source, and its sky.

The particularly modern violence of the coal mine, on the other hand, the violence that marks the activity of coal mining as determined by *Ge-Stell*, does not consist in its splitting open the earth to extract the coal – the erection of the windmill, after all, also requires splitting open the earth to lay a foundation. We can see the particularly modern violence of the coal mine in what happens after the coal is taken away from the mine. First, its relation to its location is severed when it is added to a stockpile of coal from various locations. The coal may then be used as fuel in a power plant, which, along with other plants deriving power from other sources, feeds electricity into a grid that distributes it across vast distances. The electricity that arrives at the computer on which I am writing cannot be traced to the coal or even to the coal-burning power plant; the power may come in varying proportions from coal-burning plants, nuclear reactors, even a wind turbine. The distance between me and the coal is absolutely elided in the immediate presence of its energy, in which the coal fails to show up as a thing at all. While the wind and its earth and sky are allowed to present themselves in the activity of the old windmill, the coal mine – like the new wind turbine – is part of a system in which things primarily present themselves as contributors to the grid (literally or metaphorically) of power and, having made their contributions, disappear.

Under the sway of *Ge-Stell*, in which everything shows up as its potential for the realization of will, three regions of the gathered four disappear; only the human presents itself, but not the human in its essence as 'mortal' – the one which, out of its own potential nothingness, apprehends the coming to presence of being – which, like the other three, only comes into its own in its mutual appropriation with them. Heidegger writes:

> The impression comes to prevail that everything man encounters exists only insofar as it is his construct. This illusion gives rise in turn to one final delusion: it seems as though man everywhere and always encounters only himself . . . . *In truth, however, precisely nowhere does man today any longer encounter himself, i.e., his essence.* Man stands so decisively in attendance on the challenging-forth of *Ge-Stell* that he does not apprehend *Ge-Stell* as a claim, that he fails to see himself as the one spoken to, and hence also fails in every way to hear in what respect he ek-sists, from out of his essence, in the realm of an exhortation or address, and thus *can never* encounter himself.[29]

That is to say, the threefold relationship of the human to being – belonging, listening and responding – falls by the wayside as human beings experience themselves as belonging only to the human, listening only to the human, responding only to the human.

Thus *das Ge-Stell* is *die Gefahr*, the danger, the most dangerous of all epochs of being. Heidegger writes that '*Ge-Stell* disguises [*verstellt*] the shining-forth and holding-sway of truth. The destining that sends [being] in [the form of] ordering [*Bestellen*, ordering in the sense of commanding] is consequently the extreme danger'.[30] There is an ambiguity in the word *verstellt* which is not captured by Lovitt's translation of it as 'blocks', or by Hertz's, in a similar passage in 'The way to language', as 'obstructs' (*Ge-Stell* 'obstruct[s]' *Ereignis*).[31] The latter translation, I think, is somewhat better in that it is not as strong, but both miss other senses of *verstellen* which include 'to subvert', 'to shift', 'to adjust', and – what strikes me as closest to

Heidegger's meaning – 'to disguise'.[32] Indeed, it is impossible to block or to obstruct (if this implies the possibility of prevention or even of delay) the mutual appropriation of being and human being by virtue of which being manifests in its truth. This mutual appropriation is always taking place, being is always happening to us, and happening in some way or other, whether we are aware of it or not. But whether we are aware of it or not is just what is at issue for Heidegger. *Ge-Stell* subverts the 'shining-forth and holding-sway of [the] truth [of being]', it obstructs *Ereignis*, not by keeping them from us but by making more difficult our apprehension of them as what they are – and it does so by disguising, in a particularly profound way, the very happening of being in *Ereignis*. It disguises the happening of being as something *merely human*: everything that is shows up as a projection of human will. This is the significance of Heidegger's recounting of the history of being from Descartes to Nietzsche in the fourth volume of the *Nietzsche* lectures, in which he finds a certain inevitability in the progression from Descartes, and the positing of human subjectivity as the ground on which any being must certify itself as being, to Nietzsche, and the positing of will as the being of beings.[33]

In light of this contextualization of Nietzsche's thought at the end of the history of being, we can find a new meaning in Nietzsche's figure of 'the last men'. Zarathustra describes the last man as the one who 'will no longer shoot the arrow of his longing beyond man'[34] – the last men are the last because, after the death of God, they no longer seek to transcend themselves. The time of the last men will end when the *Übermenschen* rediscover the will to transcend themselves, not towards anything higher than the human, but towards higher ideals of the human, higher ideals of their own creation. Zarathustra says that 'the earth has become small, and on it hops the last man, who makes everything small'. The earth has become small, for Nietzsche, because human beings no longer make it great through the projection of their great wills upon it. The last men will only small things; they will only their own comfort: '"We have invented happiness," say the last men, and they blink. They have left the regions where it was hard to live, for one needs warmth. One still loves one's neighbor and rubs against him, for one needs warmth.'[35]

For Nietzsche, the *Übermenschen* will make the earth great again, as an Odysseus or a Napoleon makes the earth great, by casting it as the setting of their own great wills. But on a certain wider Heideggerian view, there is no essential difference between the last men and the *Übermenschen*: the *Übermenschen*, who are also oblivious to the daimonic nature of the human, who also do not listen to the call of being but hear only themselves, are also last men. They also make the earth small, in the sense that Heidegger invokes at the beginning of 'The thing'. Indeed, in that sense, the last men and the *Übermenschen* alike do not just make the earth small – they make it disappear.

The last men say they have invented happiness in the will to comfort for themselves; the *Übermenschen* reinvent happiness in the will to self-overcoming. Both the last men and the *Übermenschen* are under the sway of *Ge-Stell*; both apprehend what is, and what they themselves are, as will and the stuff of its potential realization. Both are oblivious of deep happiness, the happiness that consists in what is fitting for human beings, which is dwelling in their fitting together with being.

Up the Creek from *Ge-Stell* to Φύσις

I am going to take you for a walk out of the city, up a creek, with Heidegger. We are going to walk backwards: backwards from one epoch to another in the history of being, from *Ge-Stell* to φύσις, to an epoch of being from which it is easier to get in view the happening of being itself, *Ereignis*. We are going to do it to show that it can be done, that it is not so difficult to take a step backwards, that we are not, after all, doomed, either to oblivion or to wait for a god to save us (as Heidegger infamously suggests, in his interview with *Der Spiegel*, is the only way out of the 'absolute technological state').[36]

It is a thesis of Heidegger's that something was lost in the translation from the Greek φύσις to the Latin *natura*, something that has remained lost to us in subsequent Western thought.[37] One of the things I want to do here is to recover a sense of what was lost, and to recover it by finding it in what we most typically think of as 'nature'. We can point the way towards what Heidegger thinks is lost by pointing out that the word φύσις, like 'technology', in the sense in which it stands for an epoch in Heidegger's history of being, does not name a thing or a set of things, but a relationship between ourselves and what there is.

I will sketch out what Heidegger holds that relationship to have been like over the next few paragraphs, and I will try to enter into it phenomenologically towards the end of this section. First, I will pause to consider a curiosity. The ancient Greek word τέχνη, the root of our 'technology', names, on Heidegger's understanding, almost a *kind* of φύσις. Τέχνη admits of various translations, of which 'art', in the very broad and by now virtually archaic sense in which 'art' can encompass 'science', may best serve my purposes for the moment. The 'art' of 'artifice' stands in our understanding as the very opposite of 'nature'. And yet we are always troubled when we try to explain why it is that human artifice is not itself natural, since, after all, it comes naturally to us.

In *An Introduction to Metaphysics*, Heidegger tells us that the sense of φύσις is already contrasted in ancient Greek thought with τέχνη, which 'means neither art nor technology but a *knowledge* . . . . Τέχνη is creating, building, in the sense of a knowing bringing-forth [*Hervor-bringen*]'.[38] He then comments parenthetically that 'it would require a special study to explain what is essentially the same in φύσις and in τέχνη'. However, we can quickly point towards what is the same. In Heidegger's interpretation, the essential sense of φύσις is *Aufgehen*, literally 'going up' or arising.[39] As he points out, the oldest Indo-European root of φύσις is *bheu-*. This root has the sense of growing or swelling, and from it are descended not only certain German words for being – *bin* and *bist* are the surviving ones – but also the English word 'being' itself, as well as the German *böse*, 'evil', and the English 'bucket'.[40] The proximate Greek root of φύσις, Heidegger points out, is φύω, which he defines as 'to arise, to be powerful, of itself to come forth to a stand and to remain in its stand'.[41] Both φύσις and τέχνη, then, have to do with coming-forth: the coming-forth of things can result from τέχνη, knowledge that brings things forth, or it can be simple φύσις, the spontaneous arising of things without the intervention of knowledge. In this sense, τέχνη is a special kind of φύσις (a proposition which is reflected vestigially in our own difficulties in maintaining a sharp distinction between the 'natural' and the 'artificial'). Indeed it must be, if Heidegger is correct that, for the Greeks (at least, the Greeks of Heraclitus's time), φύσις is not some sphere of beings – as 'nature' has been considered to be, according to Heidegger, ever since its translation out of φύσις – but 'being itself, by virtue of which beings become and remain observable'.[42] In his lecture on Heraclitus titled '*Aletheia*', Heidegger drives home the point by interpreting φύσις in the light of Heraclitus's saying 'φύσις κρύπτεσθαι φιλεῖ', commonly translated as 'nature loves to hide'. Heidegger glosses it as follows: 'the arising [*das Aufgehen*] (out of self-concealing) bestows favour on the self-concealed'.[43] The 'arising' of φύσις is fundamentally an arising out of concealment into presence.

In *An Introduction to Metaphysics*, Heidegger says that 'for the Greeks "being" basically meant . . . presence [*Anwesenheit*]'.[44] This proposition already appears in *Being and Time*.[45] But there, what is important about the fact that 'beings are grasped in their being as "presence"' is that 'they are understood with regard to a definite mode of time, the *present*'. Now, eight years later, in the midst of the 'turn' in Heidegger's thinking, the fundamental significance of the Greek determination of being as presence is no longer considered to be that beings are *in the present*, but that they are *present to us*; no longer that they are present in relation to the absences consisting in past and future, but that they are present in relation to the absence consisting in concealment. This being the case, and given that φύσις is thought as an arising out of concealment into presence, an understanding of being as φύσις is very close to an understanding of being itself. However, though it is close, it is not the same thing. As Heidegger continues, 'Greek philosophy never returned to this ground of being and to what it implies. It remained on the foreground of present things themselves [*des Anwesenden selbst*].'

If φύσις were identical with being itself, then the illustration Heidegger uses of the Greeks' understanding of φύσις – '*das Aufgehen einer Rose*', the emerging, opening-up, blooming, of a rose – would be a *metaphor* for being itself.[46] But for Heidegger's Greeks, the blooming rose is not a metaphor; it is rather a paradigm case of φύσις. The plant emerges from the ground, the bud emerges from the plant, the flower emerges from the bud, the fragrance emerges from the flower – that is how φύσις works, and φύσις is how *everything* works. Nonetheless, the experience of being as φύσις brings us closer to the experience of being itself. In the experience of being as *Ge-Stell*, I experience only my own will in negotiation with the manifestations of the wills of other human beings. But in the experience of being as φύσις, I experience the self-emergence of things presenting themselves.

If 'nature' is the home of φύσις, then 'the city' represents the height of *Ge-Stell*. Living things on city streets are highly determined by *Ge-Stell*, from the regularly planted trees, to the seasonally replaced flowers (their constant blooming defying the sky's seasons) in sidewalk planters, to the pigeons that are ignored as long as they stay out of the way. But one has to go only a short distance into a stand of trees to find a variety of life never visible from the street. The chipmunks and nuthatches there do not show up easily as part of the world made of human will. They *can* be assimilated into the world of *Ge-Stell*, in the same sort of way that, as Heidegger says, the Rhine is determined by *Ge-Stell* as an aesthetic object – chipmunks are 'cute'; we can exercise our will over them by coaxing them to eat peanuts – but they are unusual enough that, when they appear to us, the *way* they appear may, at least, not be as fully determined by *Ge-Stell*, as, for instance, the way city squirrels usually appear to us.

But not even city squirrels, indeed not even the standardized trees outside our houses, are necessarily, completely, always determined by *Ge-Stell*. The vestiges of previous epochal destinings of being always remain available in any thing. When, in a philosophical mood, we look out our window and ask what makes the tree there a tree, or that particular kind of tree, and not something else – what it is to be a tree, what treeness is – then the tree manifests itself under the sway of what Heidegger identifies as the way being showed itself in the epoch of Plato, as ἰδέα. And when, in the late spring, we are startled by the size and vibrancy of the leaves which have grown to their full size beneath our attention, the vestiges of the epoch of φύσις are shining through to us.

Opportunities for this kind of experience are rare in the city, but we don't have to go far for them to multiply. So I will take you on a short trip just past the edge of the city, to try to see how the shift from the experience of being as *Ge-Stell* to the experience of being as φύσις may take place.

I have decided to make my way up a creek which – according to my map – connects a series of ponds: a medium-sized one in a downtown park, a small one on a university campus, a large one on some 'vacant' land owned by the university, and a very large one in a conservation area on the outskirts of the city. I have gotten off the bus at the university, near the creek. I want to head towards the large pond on the conservation area, but I am disoriented; I don't see the small pond on the university campus, and I don't know which way to follow the creek, because I'm not sure which of its meandering directions is more northerly. My intuitive sense, however, is that the creek flows from the north, and so I head upstream, with a small nagging doubt that this isn't even the right creek.

As I approach the edge of campus (still not sure whether it is the northern or southern edge), I catch sight of a fish, a foot long or so, in the murky water. I guess that it's a trout, because trout are the kind of fish that are supposed to be in creeks in Ontario, though they are generally not found in cities. I watch it for a while, glimpsing another one or two as well, and then I catch sight of its tail, and I realize that it looks like a carp. I'm not sure, though; from what I know of carp, I would expect them to avoid currents. I head further upstream. I reach the edge of campus, and across the street, I see what I take to be a construction site, a shallow, level pit of bare earth, which the creek runs right through. In the distance, on the other side of the pit, but not in it, there is heavy machinery moving earth. This explains the murkiness of the water, I suppose, and I wonder why the creek has not been protected from the activity on its banks (for *Ge-Stell* also mandates the protection – that is, 'conservation' – of natural resources, which are the paradigm cases of *Bestand*).

I'm still not sure where I am. I know that, if I'm going the right way, the pond on the university land should not be much further. I cross the street. The smell of dead fish and mud, dead fish turning into mud – this smell which I had begun to notice a while ago, is much stronger now. I look down, from the sidewalk, at the creek in the shallow pit. The earth in the pit is drying and cracking. Next to where the creek disappears under the street, there is another narrow, shallow stretch of water, landlocked; apparently, perhaps, it was left behind after a rain had flooded the creek.

But in this shallow stretch of water, a fish jumps. I stare into it and see the dim shapes of several fish, like the ones I had seen in the creek back on the campus. I realize that these fish are trapped, and that they will die. I look on, disconcerted. I still don't know where I am. I get out my map. I see that the pond is supposed to be right up against the street. And now I realize that this shallow pit has not been dug out and levelled by bulldozers – the pond has been drained, and this pit is what is left of it. It is flat, apparently, because the pond was not there naturally in the first place; it was a flooded field. I look back at the landlocked stretch of water. Around its edges the hollowed-out bodies of dead carp, dissolving into the mud, emerge into view. I hadn't seen them before, but now, I couldn't miss them.

This is not the experience I had been expecting. I have come here to try to escape *Ge-Stell*, but instead, here is *Ge-Stell* in complete dominance. I go down to the pond bed, to continue heading upstream. I'm struck by how barren it is; there are hardly even any rocks. Before the pond was drained, I would have looked at the water and wondered what was down there. Now I can see: nothing was down there, apart from the carp which have now been forced downstream, and a flat expanse of mud. Now its nothingness, its having been nothing but the manifestation of some human will, is exposed, making way for the manifestation of some other human will.

I am seized by a mood of deep melancholy. This melancholy is not that state of 'great despair', in which, as Heidegger says, 'the importance fades from things and meaning obscures itself'[47] – rather the opposite. Everything is vivid, all-too-meaningful. The corpses of the fish, the cracked mud beneath my feet, the duck with its ducklings in the bulrushes at what had been (perhaps still was, when it made its nest) the edge of the pond, everything speaks to me of what should have been but isn't, and of what is instead. We may remind ourselves here of how Heidegger understands the ways in which affective states relate us to the world. Particularly pertinent is what he says in the *Nietzsche* lectures about what are there called 'passions': passion, Heidegger says, is 'the lucidly gathering grip on beings'.[48] A passion provides a lucid (*hellsichtig*) mastery, one that gathers: it masters through its lucid gathering. It is lucid in that it sees clearly the significance of things, on the basis of an understanding that gathers the situation into a whole.

A passion conduces to our seeing particular things – a word spoken by someone with whom we are angry, say – as part of a certain whole from which it derives its significance. For example, I am angered by something you say to me; in what you have said, I see (*sichten*) your mean-spiritedness light up clearly (*hell*), so that I now have a gathered view, a coherent under-standing, of you as someone mean-spirited, and on the basis of this gath-ered view, as long as I am angry at you, I will see your mean-spiritedness lit up in everything you say. But on a global level, an epochal one, passions conduce to our seeing particular things in relation to *beings as such and as a whole*, the way that being presents itself in a given epoch. When at last I recognize the drained pond bed, I see *Ge-Stell* lit up in it, and, in my melan-choly, a gathered view of *Ge-Stell* coalesces over the whole situation, lighting up in every thing I encounter in it – the fish, the ducks, the mud.

But this, thankfully, is not where I had meant to stop; still holding out hope, and now with a fresh reminder of what it is we are hoping to get away from, we continue our trek upstream, towards the last of the ponds con-nected by the creek, the one in the conservation area. Coming up to the conservation area, there is the pond, blue in the distance through the trees, but the conservation area is surrounded by a fence. Signs are posted around it saying that a user fee must be paid to enter, and that the area is under video surveillance. It is not evident where the fee might be paid, however, and, on foot, there is no way of finding it. The path I have been following beside the creek now peels away from it, running between the fence on one side and a busy road on the other. My melancholy redoubled, I continue fol-lowing the path, in the faint hope that the fence might, somewhere, some-how, open up, and I will be able to make my way down to the pond.

And suddenly that is just what happens. A yellow arrow appears on a tree, pointing the way through an open gate, down a path that branches off, through the woods, towards the pond. The warning signs, I now realize, have disappeared, and there are no longer any signs at all, apart from that yellow arrow, to indicate what I should or should not be doing here.

I turn down the path, and everything is different. I have turned in to the trees which had been on the other side of a fence, a standing-reserve of trees, ordered to stand ready for use upon payment of a fee. These trees have suddenly been given to me, released from the order in which they had been standing, for no reason that I can, practically, know, and this absurd-ity is what most prompts the change in my mood. Everything can be so heavily determined by *Ge-Stell*, and then, suddenly, a break.

Turning in to the trees, I am faced with the *depth* of the woods. My gaze is drawn out further and further, never seeming to reach a definite end.

This is not only because there are more and more trees as far as I can see. It is also because there is, in a sense, 'nothing here'. Of course, as I have said, there are many more different kinds of plants and animals here than there are to be found on the city streets, but the woods, very much unlike the city streets, are almost empty of anything that *demands* my attention: there is nothing impinging on me, challenging me, confronting me, working on me, commanding a response. Just the fence and its signs, the drain on my attention of being confronted with their challenge, had been enough to keep me from the depth of the woods; they had kept my attention shrunk back close to myself. The woods just metres away had been hardly there at all for me, but now even the distant woods have drawn near. Now my attention is freed, floating, not focused on any particular thing, but ready to be drawn by any sound or movement. I always have a sense in the woods that something is about to happen, something is about to appear, something is about to emerge from its hiddenness in the leaves or the underbrush – something, I don't know what. Everything, I sense, is *reaching out* to me, whether or not I am aware of it yet. This sense of being reached out to is, for some people, a negatively tinged one: the mood (or 'passion') of *fear* is what attunes them to the reticent reaching-out of the woods. For me, the mood is one of happiness, of openness: I am ready to *take in* what the woods offer. I am open to the self-revealing emergence of the woods. In my happiness, the woods, at last, light up for me in the mode of φύσις.

The path takes me right to the edge of the pond, to a parting in some bulrushes. The sun is shining and a gentle breeze is blowing. Shimmering, rounded ripples emerge, here and there, from the surface of the pond. The water, the pond, is arising from out of itself, literally swelling and rising into the air towards me – this is the pond presenting itself to me in the mode of φύσις – and in its arising from out of itself, it emerges into my attention, calling for my correspondence, in-flashing into my in-sight – and this is the being of the pond fulfilling itself in the happening of the mutual appropriation of its being and my capacity to receive its being. How close φύσις brings us to the thought of *Ereignis*!

I head back up the path. I stop at a large, straight, silver poplar tree growing in the path. I put my hand on it, feeling its coolness, press against it, put my arm around it, feeling its solidity. I lean against it, my arm around it, and I feel the tension in my body between my chest pressing against the tree and the earth pressing against my feet, feeling the tree growing out of the earth, emerging from the earth yet standing solid. What I am feeling is φύσις, the tree standing in its emergence.

I walk a short distance to an old lichen-encrusted picnic table, set off to the side of the path, I had seen on the way down. I sit there and look into the woods. My attention is captured by another, similar poplar tree that emerges from the woods. The tree is still. It reminds me of the *Voice of Fire* in its still, massive presence. I feel questioned by its presence, its apparent permanence. It has been here for years, emerging from the earth in which it stands; I have only just gotten here, and soon will leave, and perhaps never see it again, but it will still be here. It is here when no one is here, which is most of the time. When no one is here, it *is* still here. It is still present, growing into its presence – φύσις; it still presences, it still presents itself, here – an *Ereignis* waiting to happen! – when no one is here. Before I came, it was here, presencing but not present to anyone, and now I have come into its presencing and fit together with it. Its presencing was unfulfilled, before, since it was last fulfilled by some other human being; it did not fit together with anything that could receive it as presencing. (We might say that its presencing was partially fulfilled, insofar as the tree was present the animals of the woods, but they are not capable of receiving, and wondering at, its presencing *as* presencing.) Now I am receiving its presencing, fulfilling its being, allowing it to light up, to become manifest. I have stepped into its presencing and will step out of it again, and this enables me to dwell in its presencing, to receive its presencing as presencing. I fit together, in a relation of mutual appropriation, with the being of the tree, but I fit together in the way that I do, dwelling on my fitting together with its being, only because I have not fit together with its being before and will not fit together with its being again.

I look out into the depth of the woods again. The breeze comes up, the leaves flutter, and some smaller trees sway. I feel their movement like I am being tickled. It is the same feeling as when I am watching and listening to someone play the piano – not performing a programme, in a recital, but just playing, when I don't know what they might play, how they might play it, whether they might make mistakes or not, how they might react. The mystery of the player unfolds in the playing; I don't know what to expect, and so my expectations remain open, I await what comes, and whatever comes is *thrilling*, as long as the player spontaneously allows the mystery to unfold, allows herself to emerge in her playing. This emergence, too, is φύσις. The trees emerge from the woods in their swaying, the leaves emerge from the trees in their fluttering. The full but gentle sound of the wind in the trees begins to fade – the wind emerges in this fading sound, catching my breath as I await its disappearance or its swelling again, its disappearance out of which it might swell again.

The *thrill*, that tickling, breath-catching feeling, comes from some 'move-ment' in the being of a thing while I am fit tightly together with it, dwelling in my fitting-together with it. In that thrill I become aware of my being fit tightly together with the being of the thing, whether it is a tree or a human being. Music thrills me in the same way when I am intensely attuned to it, dwelling in my fitting together with its presence to me, and something emerges from it, subtly but strikingly, like the gentle emergence of the shimmering ripples on the water, as when a melody reaches its peak and the descant moves one semitone higher, a note's momentary emergence out of harmony – φύσις – its dissonance pressing, straining the edges of my fitting-together with the music, further opening up my connection with it – *Ereignis*.

We can see in all this how close the apprehension of being in the destin-ing of φύσις is to the apprehension of being as such, *Ereignis*: the thrill of the apprehension of being as φύσις, that sym-pathetic upwelling in which we feel bodily the upwelling of things (when the trees sway I feel myself swaying with them) emerging into presence to us, presenting themselves to us, their being fitting together with our capacity to receive it ever more intensely in their ongoing emergence, points us towards their presenting themselves to us, our fitting together with their being. The thrill of the reception of being as φύσις is not the same thing as deep happiness, but it is possible only because deep happiness is possible, and it brings us to the doorstep of deep happiness (just as, at the beginning of the history of being, it brought us to the doorstep in the other direction), by giving us a sense of the emergence of things out of their concealment to us.

Conclusion

Human beings are the only kind of beings we know of that not only fit together with being but also are capable of being aware of their fitting together with being. We can guess that there are other beings in the universe which also have these capacities, but as far as we presently know, there are not. The experiences of deep happiness described in this book's sketches are, from our everyday perspective, familiar perhaps to the point of being clichéd. But from a perspective taking into account our place, as far as we can know it, in the universe – taking into account, that is, how much there is, being, in the universe and (as far as we know) how little there is (only us!) with which being can fit together and find its fulfilment, and have its happening recognized and responded to for what it is – these experiences are dizzyingly rare.

However, the ways that we have developed to conceptualize our experience, in the Western tradition at least, conspire to occlude the rarity of such experiences, because they conspire to occlude our experience of things – in the terms of 'The turning', the reciprocal in-flashing of and in-sight into being – altogether. The occlusion of our experience of things is most complete in the view which conceives of a human being's relation to things as essentially the same as that of an information processing machine – a view which is extreme in historical terms, but very commonplace nowadays.[1] On such computationalist views, things are, for us, sources of data, which we then process and respond to; we have contact with information *about* things, but not with things themselves. But the occlusion of our experience of things also occurs in views opposed to computationalist ones – for instance, in the view of those who insist that a complete theory of mind must account for qualia. In fact, the occlusion occurs in any view following the characteristically modern Western thought that what we experience are not *things* but our *re-presentations* (which qualia are thought to be) – or in the typical postmodern term, our *constructions* – of things.

On a representationalist view, if human beings were to disappear, human beings themselves would be the only losers. But on the view I have developed in this book, if human beings were to disappear, it would be a loss for things in general: their being would no longer be fulfilled in its reception by beings capable of both receiving and reflecting on it. This means that, as human beings, we are responsible, for ourselves, not only to ourselves, but to things as well. This responsibility is not 'moral' in any usual sense; it is not a responsibility that can be weighed on the same scales as our responsibilities to treat each other justly, for instance. By 'responsible' I mean what the word says: we are able to respond, and because we are able to respond, it is incumbent upon us to consider whether and how to respond. It would not be 'wrong' in a 'moral' sense for us to decide to replace ourselves with information-processing replicas of ourselves – and if we accept a view of ourselves that holds us to be information processing machines, then we are already on the way to replacing ourselves with information-processing replicas of human beings, whether or not we build the machines – but it would be irresponsible of us to do so without facing what we would thereby be doing.

Computationalist and otherwise representationalist views of human being and its relations with things are the foundation of the 'last men's' conception of happiness. Conversely, the deep happiness that consists in our dwelling in our fitting together with the being of things is a wedge with which we may pry ourselves loose from those views of human being. Generally speaking, we all have, or at least are capable of having, experiences of this kind of happiness. The matter is to interpret and describe these experiences so that we can present in words what is most important about them, so that we are not inclined to discount them, so that we do not reduce them, or salvage in them only what is reducible, to happiness of the 'last men's' kind, and also so that we do not deny that they are experiences of anything properly called 'happiness' – which (whatever it may be) we are inclined to consider, as Aristotle considered εὐδαιμονία (whatever it may be), the natural goal of our pursuits.

It might be asked: will the proper interpretation and description of these experiences – will this book – help us to be happy? Of course, this book is concerned with something more like the philosophical question of what deep happiness is than it is with the technical question of how to achieve it. On the other hand, as Plato emphasizes, it helps to be clear about the nature of what we want before we set about trying to get it, and so clarifying what it is that we want is a good first step toward getting it. We want happiness: somehow or other, this is true for all of us – a truism, as Aristotle says. What we, today, typically mean by 'happiness' is the happiness of desire-satisfaction. At a higher level of abstraction, we mean that we want that beyond which we would want nothing else. This way of putting it – beyond which we would *want* nothing else – prejudices our view of happiness toward desire-satisfaction: if I want to be happy, then I catalogue my wants and set about fulfilling them; the more I fulfil, the happier I am, and when none are left outstanding, when I can think of nothing else that I want, then I am happy.

I *must* be happy, or *should* be happy – but as is all too familiar to many of us, it very often happens that when we have fulfilled all the desires we thought we had, we still are not happy. For some of us, this may be in part because our desires were not fitting for us; we had adopted the desires of others as our own. Not knowing what we want ourselves, we do not know how to become happy even in the sense of desire-satisfaction. Trapped in this dilemma, the only apparent ways out may be medication or a form of psychotherapy that aims to make us into the people we thought we were, the people for whom what we wanted is, indeed, fitting.

If those efforts are successful, then we may become happier, perhaps as happy as people generally are, who have wants that are fitting for them and who take satisfaction in the fulfilment of those wants. They may indeed want nothing else for themselves; they may indeed consider themselves happy; they may indeed *be* happy. And, being happy in this way, they may also recognize that there are those moments – they might call them bliss, joy, euphoria – such as I have described in the sketches in this book, and of course they will recognize them as desirable. In fact they may intensely crave such moments, and they may even imagine that their happiness depends on them, especially those moments having to do with connection with other human beings. But, typically, we assimilate our craving for these moments to the collection of desires whose satisfaction, we suppose, makes us happy. As a result of this assimilation, we think that the satisfaction of one desire is as good as the satisfaction of another: as people often say, for instance, good chocolate is better than sex.

When the kinds of experiences examined in this book's sketches are described in terms of desire-satisfaction, they lose their particularity. When they are described in those terms, the happiness involved in them is seen to have nothing in particular to do with the nature of the experience itself, as opposed to the satisfaction of the desire occasioning it. Described in the terms developed over the course of this book, however, these experiences are different in kind from ordinary experiences of desire-satisfaction; they are experiences of what is fitting for us as human beings, no matter who or where or when we happen to be.

For the Heidegger of *Being and Time*, it is important for the philosopher to attend to *Angst* – not necessarily to cultivate it, for it is always with us – in order to come to a phenomenological understanding of *Da-Sein*'s temporality, and so to be able to discover the meaning of being, that it is a temporal happening. Following the later Heidegger, to attend to deep happiness is important not only for the philosopher (or 'thinker') but for human beings generally, because it allows us the opportunity to rediscover being's happening to us in our fitting together with being, which has been forgotten since the beginning of Western thought and has become ever more distant from our thinking through the successive epochs of being. The proper understanding of our fitting together with being, in turn, will help to ensure that we do not allow opportunities for deep happiness to be closed off.

Glossary

This is a rough-and-ready guide to some important Greek and German words appearing in this book. There is controversy over the meanings of many of these terms.

Greek

ἀλήθεια (*alētheia*) – 'truth' (glossed by Heidegger as 'unconcealedness')
ἀπάθεια (*apatheia*) – lack of emotion
ἀρχή (*archē*) – beginning, ground, founding principle
δαίμων (*daimōn*) – divine or semi-divine being, between humans and gods
δικαιοσύνη (*dikaiosunē*) – the virtue of 'justice'
δίκη (*dikē*) – 'justice'
εἶδος (*eidos*) – 'form', as in Plato; also 'appearance'
ἔργον (*ergon*) – 'function'
Ἔρως (*Erōs*) – the daimonic personification of eros, 'love'
εὐδαιμονία (*eudaimonia*), adj. = εὐδαίμων – 'happiness'
ἡδονή (*hēdonē*) – 'pleasure'
θεορία (*theoria*) – 'contemplation'
θεός (*theos*) – 'god'
ἰδέα (*idea*), plural ἰδέαι – 'idea', 'form', as in Plato; also 'appearance'
λόγος (*logos*) – 'reason', 'rationality', 'language'
νοῦς (*nous*) – 'reason', 'understanding'
πάθος (*pathos*) – 'feeling'
τέλος (*telos*) – 'end', 'goal'
τέχνη (*technē*) – theoretical know-how
φύσις (*phusis*) – 'nature'

German

Befindlichkeit – 'way of being attuned'
Da-Sein – literally 'being here/there'; the early Heidegger's term for human existence

Ereignis – in ordinary German, 'event'; in Heidegger's technical usage after the 'turn', translated as '(event of) appropriation' or 'enowning': the happening of being in the mutual appropriation between being and human being

Ge-Stell – the be-setting 'framing' of modern technology: Heidegger's name for the latest epoch in the history of being

Gott – 'god'

Gottheit – 'godhead'; god-ness, divinity, the holy

Göttlichen – 'divinities'

Grundstimmung – 'basic/grounding mood'

das Man – the 'one' or 'they', as in 'they say' or 'one doesn't do that'

Sein – 'being'

Seinsvergessenheit/Seynsvergessenheit – 'oblivion of being' or 'forgetting of being'

Seinsverlassenheit/Seynsverlassenheit – 'abandonment of being'

Seyn – the archaic spelling of *Sein* by which Heidegger after the 'turn' (mostly in works not published in his lifetime) indicates being in the sense of *Ereignis*

Stimmung – 'mood'

Unheimlichkeit – 'uncanniness'; more literally, not-at-home-ness

Notes

Introduction

[1] *Was-sein* is translated as 'what-being' in Heidegger, 'On the question of being', in *Pathmarks*, ed. William McNeill (New York: Cambridge University Press, 1998), 315; it is translated as 'whatness' in Heidegger, 'Metaphysics as history of being: Whatness and thatness in the essential beginning of metaphysics', in *The End of Philosophy*, tr. Joan Stambaugh (Chicago: Chicago University Press, 2003).

[2] This has its purest expression in Kant's response to the ontological argument, namely, that to say 'x is' means nothing, because *that* x is is taken for granted once we say *what* x is.

[3] Heidegger, *What is Called Thinking?*, tr. J. Glenn Gray (New York: Harper & Row, 1968), 30. Note that I frequently modify translations from German and Greek; where I do so, I give references to both the translation and the original.

[4] Quoted in Heidegger, *What is Called Thinking?*, 64.

[5] Note that I follow recent translations of Heidegger including Stambaugh's translation of *Being and Time* in writing 'being', where it renders Heidegger's *Sein*, with a lower-case 'b'. The older convention of capitalizing it strikes me as conducive to what, for Heidegger, is the fundamental error of metaphysics, that is, thinking of being as a being.

[6] See John Searle's famous 'Chinese room' article, 'Minds, brains, and programs', in *The Nature of Mind*, ed. David M. Rosenthal (New York: Oxford University Press, 1991), particularly the amazingly but unfortunately not surprisingly obtuse objections that Searle reports. In analytic philosophy of mind, which retains the dichotomy of subject and object, the oblivion of being seems to me to show up, not quite as itself, but as the denial of intentionality and/or qualia.

[7] Heidegger, *Being and Time*, tr. Joan Stambaugh (Albany: State University of New York Press, 1996), 167. References to *Being and Time* are to Stambaugh's translation unless otherwise noted; citations refer to the original German pagination, found in the margins.

[8] Heidegger, *An Introduction to Metaphysics*, tr. Ralph Manheim (New York: Anchor Books, 1961), 10.

[9] Heidegger, 'Only a god can save us: *Der Spiegel*'s interview with Martin Heidegger', tr. Maria P. Alter and John D. Caputo, *Philosophy Today* 20 (1976): 267–285, 276. This is not the place to deal with the shocking applications Heidegger makes of some of the categories and vocabulary of *Being and Time* during the period of his rectorship in Freiburg, but I would say that it seems clear to me that his view of the relationship between politics and philosophy during that period (whatever his political views were before and after) was a brief aberration.

[10] Medard Boss, 'Martin Heidegger's Zollikon Seminars', tr. Brian Kenny, *Review of Existential Psychology and Psychiatry* 16 (1979): 7–20, 7.

[11] Heidegger, 'Letter on "humanism"', in *Pathmarks*, ed. William McNeill (New York: Cambridge University Press, 1998), 252; GA 9, 331. Note that references to the *Gesamtausgabe* will take this form: GA followed by the volume number.

[12] Heidegger, *Nietzsche, Volume III: The Will to Power as Knowledge and as Metaphysics*, ed. David Farrell Krell, tr. Joan Stambaugh, David Farrell Krell and Frank A. Capuzzi. (New York: HarperCollins, 1991), 4.

[13] Heidegger, 'What is metaphysics?', in *Pathmarks*, ed. William McNeill (New York: Cambridge University Press, 1998), 15. See also Heidegger, *The Fundamental Concepts of Metaphysics: World, Finitude, Solitude*, tr. William McNeill and Nicholas Walker (Bloomington: Indiana University Press, 1995), 56: 'Whenever we survey our whole discussion of the concept of metaphysics, we see that this title expresses a knowledge that is directed toward *beings as a whole.*'

[14] Heidegger, *What is Called Thinking?*, 50; GA 8, 53.

[15] Heidegger, 'Time and being', in *On Time and Being*, tr. Joan Stambaugh (Chicago: University of Chicago Press, 2002), 9; GA 14, 13.

[16] Heidegger, *Contributions to Philosophy (From Enowning)*, tr. Parvis Emad and Kenneth Maly (Bloomington: Indiana University Press, 1999), 330; GA 65, 470.

[17] Heidegger, 'The way to language', in *On the Way to Language*, tr. Peter D. Hertz (New York: HarperCollins, 1982), 129n.

[18] Cf. 'Time and being', 23–24.

[19] Heidegger, 'The turning', in *The Question Concerning Technology and Other Essays*, tr. William Lovitt (New York: Harper Torchbooks, 1977), 38–39; GA 79, 69.

[20] Heidegger, 'The onto-theo-logical constitution of metaphysics', in *Identity and Difference*, tr. Joan Stambaugh with original German (Chicago: University of Chicago Press, 2002), 64/132.

[21] Quoted in S. Marc Cohen, Patricia Curd and C. D. C. Reeve, eds, *Readings in Ancient Greek Philosophy From Thales to Aristotle*, 2nd edn (Indianapolis: Hackett Publishing Company, 2000), 6.

[22] See Heidegger, *Basic Concepts*, tr. Gary E. Aylesworth (Bloomington: Indiana University Press, 1993); Heidegger, 'The Anaximander fragment', in *Early Greek Thinking*, tr. David Farrell Krell and Frank A. Capuzzi. New York: Harper and Row, 1984; Heidegger, 'Anaximander's saying' in *Off the Beaten Track*, ed. and tr. Julian Young and Kenneth Haynes (New York: Cambridge University Press, 2002).

[23] H. G. Liddell and R. Scott, eds, *Greek-English Lexicon* (New York: Oxford University Press, 1996), s.v. 'δίκη'.

[24] Heidegger, *Basic Concepts*, 85.

[25] Though I will speak here as if human beings are unique in this regard, I will not speculate as to whether this is a characteristic *only* of human beings. The terms '*Da-Sein*' and 'mortals' which Heidegger uses in his earlier and later periods have the advantage of not pre-judging this point, but they have the disadvantage of obscuring the fact that the kind of beings referred to include ordinary human beings; they can have the effect of preventing the reader from feeling that she or he is implicated in the discussion. To speak of *Da-Sein* makes it sound like we are talking about somebody else. To speak of human beings, hopefully, helps us

to remember that we are talking about ourselves, something which is important to remember for our purposes here.

26 Heidegger, *Being and Time*, 54.

27 Heidegger, *Being and Time*, 54.

28 Heidegger, *Being and Time*, 55.

29 Heidegger develops these notions in a somewhat different direction in *The Fundamental Concepts of Metaphysics* – a lecture course given on the cusp of the 'turn' – where he characterizes human being as 'world-forming', animal being as 'poor in world' and inanimate being as 'worldless'. See Heidegger, *The Fundamental Concepts of Metaphysics*, Part 2.

30 Heidegger, *Being and Time*, 138.

31 Heidegger, *Being and Time*, 188.

32 Heidegger, *Being and Time*, 188–189.

33 Heidegger, *Being and Time*, 189.

34 Heidegger, 'Building dwelling thinking', in *Poetry, Language, Thought*, tr. Albert Hofstadter (New York: Haper & Row, 1975), 149–151; *Vorträge und Aufsätze, Teil 2* (Tübingen: Günther Neske Pfullingen, 1967), 23–25.

35 See especially Heidegger, 'Building dwelling thinking', 150.

36 Heidegger, 'Building dwelling thinking', 148.

37 Heidegger, *Hölderlin's Hymn 'The Ister'*, tr. William McNeill and Julia Davis (Bloomington: Indiana University Press, 1996), 54.

38 For the Macquarrie and Robinson translation, see Heidegger, *Being and Time*, tr. John Macquarrie and Edward Robinson (New York : Harper and Row, 1962).

39 Hubert L. Dreyfus, *Being-in-the-World: A Commentary on Heidegger's* Being and Time, *Division 1* (Cambridge, MA: MIT Press, 1991), 168.

40 One problem that arises in translating *Befindlichkeit* as 'affectedness' is that it seems odd to use it as a count noun, as in formulations such as '*Angst* is an affectedness' (though we do use words such as 'illness' that way). This may point toward an ambiguity in Heidegger's concept of *Befindlichkeit*: on one hand, *Befindlichkeit* refers to the ontological fact that being is always (experienced as) affected; on the other hand, it refers to particular *ways* of being affected, that is, to different affective states. In any event, we shall use 'affectedness' to refer to *Befindlichkeit* in the first sense and 'way of being affected' to refer to *Befindlichkeit* in the second sense.

41 Heidegger, *Being and Time*, 137.

42 Heidegger, *Being and Time*, 138.

43 Note that the distinction is particularly unclear between *Stimmung* and what I have identified as the second sense of *Befindlichkeit*. Notwithstanding my explication of *Angst* as a *Befindlichkeit* here, Heidegger often seems to write of *Angst* as if it were a *Stimmung*, that is, as if it were a particular ontic state rather than a general ontological feature of *Da-Sein*.

44 Heidegger, *Being and Time*, 188–190.

45 Stambaugh uses 'anxiety' to render *Bangigkeit*, which Heidegger lists among the 'variations of fear [*Furcht*]'. Heidegger, *Being and Time*, 142.

46 Notice the tension in this formulation: if the phenomenon is defined as that which presents itself to us, how can we discern and describe anything *but* phenomena? This tension may be why Heidegger discarded the ontic/ontological distinction shortly after *Being and Time*. See Heidegger, *The Fundamental Concepts of Metaphysics*, 360.

47 Heidegger, *Being and Time*, 137.

48 Perhaps as a result of Heidegger's renunciation of the ontic/ontological distinction in *The Fundamental Concepts of Metaphysics*, the word *Grundstimmung* appears in that work where *Being and Time* would have led us to expect *Grundbefindlichkeit*.

49 Heidegger, *Nietzsche, Volume I*, 45; *Nietzsche, Erster Band* (Tübingen: Verlag Günther Neske Pfullingen, 1961), 56.

50 Heidegger, *Nietzsche I*, 47.

51 Heidegger, *Nietzsche I*, 47–48.

52 Heidegger, *Nietzsche I*, 45–46.

53 Heidegger, *Nietzsche I*, 48; *Nietzsche, Erster Band*, 59.

54 Heidegger, *Nietzsche I*, 48.

55 Heidegger, *Being and Time*, 134.

56 Heidegger, *Nietzsche I*, 49.

57 Heidegger, *Nietzsche I*, 49.

58 Heidegger, *Nietzsche I*, 51.

59 Heidegger, *Nietzsche I*, 52; Heidegger, *Nietzsche, Erster Band*, 64.

60 In French (as the lecture was given in France) Heidegger adds parenthetically, '*nous touche*'.

61 Heidegger, *What is Philosophy?*, tr. William Kluback and Jean T. Wilde with German original (New York: Twayne Publishers, 1958), 23.

62 Heidegger, *What is Philosophy?*, 25.

63 Heidegger, *What is Philosophy?*, 77.

64 Heidegger, *What is Philosophy?*, 77–79.

65 At the time of that lecture course, however, the change in Heidegger's conception of the happening of being had not yet occurred: boredom is a fundamental attunement because, like *Angst*, it affords us an insight into the temporality of our existence and thereby into the meaning of being in general.

66 Heidegger, *Contributions to Philosophy*, 32.

67 Heidegger, *What is Philosophy?*, 79–81.

68 Heidegger, *What is Philosophy?*, 87.

69 Heidegger, *What is Philosophy?*, 89–91.

70 Heidegger, *What is Philosophy?*, 91. Though Heidegger does not mention it in this text, he evidently is referring to the mood belonging to what he calls '*das Ge-Stell*', technological 'enframement'. I will examine *das Ge-Stell* in Chapter 4.

71 In this way it is related to 'startled dismay', as I will explain in Chapter 3.

Chapter 1

1 'Εὐδαιμονία ἐστὶ δαίμων ἀγαθός.' Marcus Aurelius Antoninus, *The Communings with Himself of Marcus Aurelius Antoninus*, Loeb Classical Library edn, tr. C. R. Haines with original Greek (Cambridge, MA: Harvard University Press, 1961), VII.17. Cf. H. G. Liddell and R. Scott, *Greek-English Lexicon*, s.v. εὐδαιμοσύνη.

2 James Morwood and John Taylor, eds, *Pocket Oxford Classical Greek Dictionary* (Oxford: Oxford University Press, 2002), s.v. 'δαίμων'. Δαίμων can also mean 'fate'.

3 'Πᾶν τό δαιμόνιον μεταξύ ἐστι θεοῦ τε καὶ θνητοῦ.' Plato, *Symposium*, tr. H. N. Fowler with Greek original (Cambridge, MA: Harvard University Press, 1914), 202e.

4   Plato, *Timaeus*, Loeb Classical Library edn, tr. R. G. Bury with Greek original (Cambridge, MA: Harvard University Press, 1961), 90a.

5   Plato, *Timaeus*, 90c.

6   Aurelius, *Communings*, II.13, II.17, III.3, V.27.

7   Plato, *Apology*, Loeb Classical Library edn, tr. H. N. Fowler with Greek original (Cambridge, MA: Harvard University Press, 1914), 31c–d; Plato, *Republic*, Loeb Classical Library edn, tr. Paul Shorey with Greek original (Cambridge, MA: Harvard University Press, 1937), 496c.

8   Plato, *Phaedrus*, Loeb Classical Library edn, tr. H. N. Fowler with Greek original (Cambridge, MA: Harvard University Press, 1914), 242c.

9   Plato, *Phaedrus*, tr. R. Hackforth, in *Collected Dialogues*, ed. Edith Hamilton (Princeton: Princeton University Press, 1961).

10 This claim is controversial among scholars. The best recent resource for opposing views is Pierre Destrée and Nicholas D. Smith, eds, *Socrates' Divine Sign: Religion, Practice, and Value in Socratic Philosophy* (Kelowna, BC: Academic Printing and Publishing, 2005).

11 Plato, *Apology*, 31d; *Phaedrus*, 242c.

12 Heidegger, *Being and Time*, 273.

13 Heidegger, *Contributions to Philosophy (From Enowning)*, §191. Of course, I do not mean to suggest that Heidegger accepts such a distinction between the 'earthly' or 'merely physical' and the 'divine' as either the ancients or we ourselves ordinarily might draw; the point here is just to show the resonance between Heidegger's account of *Da-Sein* and the ancients' notion of our daimonic relation with the divine.

14 Heraclitus of Ephesus, *Fragments*, tr. T. M. Robinson with Greek original (Toronto: University of Toronto Press, 1987), 68–69; cf. S. Marc Cohen, Patricia Curd and C. D. C. Reeve, eds, *Readings in Ancient Greek Philosophy From Thales to Aristotle*, 34.

15 Heidegger, 'Letter on "humanism"', 269.

16 *Pocket Oxford Classical Greek Dictionary*, s.v. 'ἦθος'. The third cluster, in which ἦθος is roughly synonymous with ἔθος, includes 'custom' and 'morality'.

17 It may be significant in this regard that, as C. de Heer points out, Homer refers to the gods as δαίμονες, but Hesiod no longer does so, while εὐδαιμονία appears in Hesiod but not Homer. C. de Heer, *Makar—Eudaimon—Olbios—Eutuchis: A Study of the Semantic Field Denoting Happiness in Ancient Greek to the End of the 5th Century B.C.* (Amsterdam: Adolf M. Hakkert, 1969), 24.

18 Heidegger, *Parmenides*, tr. André Schuwer and Richard Rojcewicz (Bloomington: Indiana University Press, 1992), 102–109.

19 Heidegger, *Parmenides*, 108–109.

20 J. L. Ackrill, 'Aristotle on *eudaimonia*', in *Essays on Aristotle's Ethics*, ed. Amélie Oksenberg Rorty (Berkeley: University of California Press, 1980), 27.

21 Aristotle, *Nicomachean Ethics*, 1177b, 1178a.

22 Aristotle, *Nicomachean Ethics*, 1178a.

23 Some commentators have questioned the translation of δικαιοσύνη as 'justice', since 'justice', in ordinary contemporary usage, has a primarily juridical sense. The juridical sense is even already dominant in its Latin root, *jūs*. *Oxford English Dictionary*, 2nd edn (New York: Oxford University Press, 1989), s.vv. 'justice', 'just'. But if we hear in 'justice' the sense of 'just' as in the phrases 'just so' and

'just right' – that is, the sense of 'no more and no less than required', or in other words, *fittingly* – then it may, in fact, bring out more of the range of δικαιοσύνη.

24 We may note that one of the several translations of ἀρετή is 'fitness' – thus we may say that δικαιοσύνη is what is *fitting* for us. *Pocket Oxford Classical Greek Dictionary*, s.v. ἀρετή; see also ἀρετάω, which is cognate with ἀρετή, and one translation of which is 'fit'; cf. Liddell and Scott, *Greek-English Lexicon*, s.v. ἀρήγω, which primarily means 'aid' or 'succour', but which also can mean 'good' or 'fit', though it is likely not etymologically cognate with ἀρετή.

25 Plato, *Republic*, 352e–354a.

26 Plato, *Republic*, 372c–373e.

27 Butler, 'The arguments for the most pleasant life in *Republic* IX', *Apeiron* 32 (1999): 37–48, 47.

28 Plato, *Republic*, 582a–d.

29 John Stuart Mill, *Utilitarianism* (Toronto: Broadview Press, 2000), 18.

30 Mill, *Utilitarianism*, 16.

31 Plato, *Republic*, 585c.

32 Plato, *Republic*, 476e–478e.

33 Plato, *Republic*, 585c.

34 Plato, *Republic*, 585e.

35 Plato, *Republic*, 586a.

36 Plato, *Republic*, 585d.

37 Plato, *Republic*, 586d–e.

38 Plato, *Republic*, 586e–587a.

39 Plato, *Republic*, 420b and 519e.

40 Robert Nozick, *The Examined Life: Philosophical Meditations* (New York: Simon and Schuster, 1989), 108.

41 Nozick, *The Examined Life*, 114.

42 L. W. Sumner, *Welfare, Happiness, and Ethics*, (New York: Clarendon Press, 1996), 143–145.

43 L. W. Sumner, 'Happiness now and then', *Apeiron* 35, no. 4 (December 2002): 21–39, 27.

44 John Locke, *Essay Concerning Human Understanding* (Oxford: Clarendon Press, 1956), II.21.42.

45 Wladyslaw Tatarkiewicz, *Analysis of Happiness*, tr. Edward Rothert and Danuta Zielinskn (The Hague: Martinus Nijhoff, 1976), 33–34. Of course, as Tatarkiewicz's book was originally written in Polish, it cannot treat happiness in our specific sense.

46 Thomas Hobbes, *Leviathan*, ed. C. B. Macpherson (New York: Penguin, 1985), 129.

47 Hobbes, *Leviathan*, 160. Bentham devotes a chapter of *Deontology* to ridiculing the idea of a *summum bonum* – the chapter is titled '*Summum bonum*: consummate nonsense' – and the ancient and medieval philosophers for believing that there might be such a thing. Jeremy Bentham, *Deontology, Together with a Table of the Springs of Action and Articles on Utilitarianism*, in *Collected Works of Jeremy Bentham*, ed. Amnon Goldworth (New York: Oxford University Press, 1983), 134–147.

48 Hobbes, *Leviathan*, 85.

49 Hobbes, *Leviathan*, 160. From Hobbes it is a short step to the metaphysic of the will to power as Heidegger interprets it in Nietzsche, which has it that 'power is

power only when and only so long as it remains power-enhancement and commands for itself "more power".' Heidegger, 'The word of Nietzsche: "God is dead"', in *The Question Concerning Technology and Other Essays*, tr. William Lovitt (New York: Harper Torchbooks, 1977), 78. We will see how Heidegger's Nietzsche relates to the modern conception of happiness and my attempt to get beyond it in Chapter 4.

50 Sumner and Richard Kraut both argue that happiness cannot be objective in the way Aristotle claims εὐδαιμονία is, from which Sumner concludes that εὐδαιμονία should not be translated as 'happiness', while Kraut concludes that Aristotle is wrong about εὐδαιμονία/happiness. See Richard Kraut, 'Two conceptions of happiness', *Philosophical Review* 88, no. 2 (April 1979): 167–197.

51 Kraut, 'Two conceptions of happiness', 177.

52 Sumner, 'Happiness now and then', 30.

53 Sumner, 'Happiness now and then', 24.

54 Sumner, 'Happiness now and then', 25.

55 Sumner, 'Happiness now and then', 28.

56 Sumner, 'Happiness now and then', 28.

Chapter 2

1 This has been perhaps most helpfully explained by Thomas Sheehan, 'A paradigm shift in Heidegger research', *Continental Philosophy Review* 32, no. 2 (2001): 1–20.

2 See Sheehan, 'A paradigm shift in Heidegger research', 13–14. Sheehan draws our attention to Heidegger's differentiation between *die Kehre* and *die Wendung* in Heidegger's letter to Richardson, published as the preface to William J. Richardson, *Heidegger: Through Phenomenology to Thought* (New York: Fordham University Press, 2003), viii–xxiii.

3 As Heidegger also makes clear in his letter to Richardson, what he had in mind as '*die Kehre*' was not a turning that he himself was to carry out; what he was to carry out was rather the *thinking* of the turning.

4 See, for instance, Steven Galt Crowell, 'Metaphysics, metontology, and the end of *Being and Time*', in Hubert L. Dreyfus and Mark Wrathall, eds, *Heidegger Reexamined, Volume I: Dasein, Authenticity, and Death* (New York: Routledge, 2002), 345–369. Crowell offers both highly abstract reasons, having to do with Heidegger's engagement with and disengagement from Kant and transcendental philosophy, and political ones, having to do with the 'decisionism' that supposedly gripped Heidegger at the beginning of his National Socialist period.

5 See Heidegger, *Nietzsche, Volume II: The Eternal Recurrence of the Same*, ed. and tr. David Farrell Krell (New York: HarperCollins, 1991).

6 Heidegger, 'Letter on "humanism"', 250.

7 Heidegger, 'Letter on "humanism"', 250.

8 Heidegger, *The Basic Problems of Phenomenology*, tr. Albert Hofstadter (Bloomington: Indiana University Press, 1988), §19.

9 Heidegger, 'The turning', in *The Question Concerning Technology and Other Essays*, tr. William Lovitt (New York: Harper Torchbooks, 1977), 44 (emphasis added).

10 Heidegger, 'The turning', 46.

11 Sheehan, 'A paradigm shift in Heidegger research', 14–15.

12 Heidegger, 'The principle of identity', in *Identity and Difference*, tr. Joan Stambaugh with German original (Chicago: University of Chicago Press, 2002), 36/100. For another example, Heidegger places his discussion of *Ereignis* in 'The way to language' under the following heading: 'The moving force in Showing of Saying is Owning' (*'Das Regende im Zeigen der Sage ist das Eignen'*). Heidegger, 'The way to language', in *On the Way to Language*, tr. Peter D. Hertz (New York: HarperCollins, 1982), 127; GA 12, 246.

13 Sheehan, 'A paradigm shift in Heidegger research', 20.

14 Heidegger, *Identity and Difference*, 100–101.

15 Heidegger also invokes the connection between *Ereignis* and *äugen* in 'The way to language': '*Ereignis* appropriates [*ereignet*] in its beholding [*Er-äugnen*] of the human essence of mortals, through which it appropriates [*vereignet*] them to what it avows *to* [zu*sagt*] humans in the saying [*Sage*] from everywhere out of the concealed.' Heidegger, 'The way to language', 129; GA 12, 249.

16 Heidegger, *Identity and Difference*, 36/100.

17 Heidegger, 'The turning', 45–46.

18 Heidegger, 'The principle of identity', 37/102. Stambaugh translates *schwingende* with 'vibrating', which seems to add an unnecessary obscurity.

19 Heidegger, 'Time and being', 14–15.

20 Heidegger, 'Time and being', 17; GA 14, 22.

21 Heidegger, 'Time and being', 19.

22 Heidegger, 'Letter on "humanism"', 145n.

23 Heidegger, *Contributions to Philosophy*, 307.

24 Heidegger, 'A dialogue on language', in *On the Way to Language*, tr. Peter D. Hertz (New York: HarperCollins, 1982), 19.

25 Heidegger, 'On the essence of truth', in *Pathmarks*, ed. William McNeill (New York: Cambridge University Press, 1998), 96–97; GA 9, 96–97.

26 GA 40, *passim* and 219–230; GA 79, 68–77, cf. Heidegger, *Die Technik und die Kehre* (Tübingen: Neske, 1962).

27 See, for instance, 'The onto-theo-logical constitution of metaphysics', 73.

28 For instance, Heidegger, 'Letter on "humanism"', 146n and 147n, respectively.

29 Heidegger, 'Letter on "humanism"', 148 and 148n.

30 Heidegger, *Being and Time*, 215.

31 Heidegger, 'Letter on "humanism"', 239.

32 Heidegger, 'A dialogue on language', 5.

33 Heidegger, *What is Called Thinking?*, 130.

34 I examine Heidegger's etymological method in more detail in 'Heidegger's etymological method: Discovering being by recovering the richness of the word', *Philosophy Today* 51, no. 3 (2007): 278–289.

35 Heidegger, *What is Called Thinking?*, 139–140.

36 Heidegger, *Being and Time*, 170.

37 Heidegger, *Being and Time*, 169.

38 Heidegger, 'The nature of language', in *On the Way to Language*, tr. Peter D. Hertz (New York: HarperCollins, 1982), 76.

39 Heidegger, 'The nature of language', 88.

[40] Heidegger, *Being and Time*, 220.

[41] See, for instance, Heidegger, *An Introduction to Metaphysics*, 11.

[42] Heidegger, *An Introduction to Metaphysics*, 11.

[43] Jacques Derrida, *Speech and Phenomena and Other Essays on Husserl's Theory of Signs*, tr. David B. Allison (Evanston, IL: Northwestern University Press, 1973), 159–160.

[44] Heidegger, 'The Anaximander Fragment', 52.

[45] Heidegger, *An Introduction to Metaphysics*, 61.

[46] Frank Schalow, 'Language and the etymological turn of thought', *Graduate Faculty Philosophy Journal* 18, no. 1 (1995): 187–203, 196.

[47] Schalow, 'Language and the etymological turn of thought', 197.

[48] Daniel M. Haybron, 'What do we want from a theory of happiness?', *Metaphilosophy* 34, no. 3 (April 2003): 305–328, 306. Of course, if happiness and associated concepts were well-defined and univocal, there would be no call for their analysis in the first place.

[49] Consider a simple example: many English speakers now use the phrase 'in lieu of' to mean 'in light of'. Perhaps not everyone who uses it that way would be swayed by its being pointed out that *lieu* means 'place' in French, but I suspect most would.

[50] *Oxford English Dictionary*, 2nd edn (New York: Oxford University Press, 1989), s.v. 'hap'.

[51] *Oxford English Dictionary*, 2nd edn, s.v. 'happy', 'hap'; C.T. Onions ed. *Oxford Dictionary of English Etymology* (Oxford: Clarendon, 1969), s.v. 'hap'; Eric Partridge, *Origins: A Short Etymological Dictionary of Modern English* (New York: Macmillan, 1966), s.v. 'hap'; Ernest Klein, *A Comprehensive Etymological Dictionary of the English Language*, (Amsterdam: Elsevier, 1966), s.v. 'hap'.

[52] Robert Claiborne, ed., *Roots of English* (New York: TimesBooks, 1978), s.v. 'KOB'.

[53] *Oxford Dictionary of English Etymology*, s.v. 'hap'; Klein, *A Comprehensive Etymological Dictionary*, s.v. 'hap'.

[54] Kraut, 'Two conceptions of happiness', 188.

[55] John Wilson, 'Happiness', *Analysis* 29 (1968): 13–21, 13.

[56] *Oxford English Dictionary*, 2nd edn, s.v. 'happy'.

[57] Ninian Smart, 'What is happiness?', in *The Good Life and its Pursuit*, ed. Jude P. Dougherty (New York: Paragon House, 1984), 36.

[58] Notice that the French *heureux* literally means 'timely'.

[59] The word 'felicity', of course, is derived from the Latin *felix*; the root of the latter word, *fe*, comes from the Proto-Indo-European root *dhe*, which originally means 'to suck' or 'to suckle', and which acquired by association meanings relating to nourishment and fruitfulness. Thus 'felicity' shares its root with, for instance, 'fecund' and 'female'. See Harper, *The Online Etymological Dictionary*, http://www.etymonline.com/index.php?term=fecund, http://www.etymonline.com/index.php?term=felicity, and http://www.etymonline.com/index.php? term=female.

[60] J. L. Austin, *How to Do Things with Words*, ed. J. O. Urmson and Marina Sbisà (Oxford: Clarendon Press, 1975), 13–14.

[61] Kraut, 'Two conceptions of happiness', 186n–187n.

[62] Roger Montague, 'Happiness', *Proceedings of the Aristotelian Society* 67 (1967): 87–102, 97.

63 See, for instance, Dreyfus and Haugeland, 'Husserl and Heidegger: Philosophy's last stand', in *Heidegger and Modern Philosophy*, ed. Michael Murray (New Haven: Yale University Press, 1978), 231.

64 Heidegger, 'My way to phenomenology', in *On Time and Being*, tr. Joan Stambaugh (Chicago: University of Chicago Press, 2002), 82. Here Heidegger echoes the following passage in *Being and Time*: 'Our elucidations of the preliminary concept of phenomenology show that its essential character does not consist in its *actuality* as a philosophical "movement." Higher than actuality stands *possibility*. We can understand phenomenology solely by seizing on it as a possibility.' Heidegger, *Being and Time*, 38.

65 Heidegger, *Being and Time*, 28.

66 Heidegger, 'The nature of language', 63.

67 Heidegger, 'Language in the poem', in *On the Way to Language*, 166.

68 Heidegger, 'The thing', in *Poetry, Language, Thought*, tr. Albert Hofstadter (New York: Harper and Row, 1975), 166.

69 Heidegger, 'The thing', 166.

70 Heidegger, 'The thing', 177.

71 Heidegger, 'Time and being', 2; see David Farrell Krell, *Intimations of Mortality* (University Park, PA: Pennsylvania State University Press, 1986), 103, for a reassurance from Heidegger that he does not mean to say that there is being without beings.

72 Recall again Heidegger's remark about 'the point' of the dialogue with poetry: we want 'to undergo an experience with language', which is to say: we want, through language, to *share* an experience.

73 Heidegger, 'Time and being', 2.

74 Heidegger, 'The way to language', 115.

75 The authoritative text is to be found in Robert Frost, *The Poetry of Robert Frost*, ed. Edward Connery Lathem (New York: Henry Holt and Company, 1979).

76 Heidegger, 'The nature of language', 63.

77 Heidegger, 'Language', in *Poetry, Language, Thought*, tr. Albert Hofstadter (New York: Harper & Row, 1975), 190; GA 12, 10.

Chapter 3

1 See Heidegger, 'Memorial address', in *Discourse on Thinking*, tr. John M. Anderson and E. Hans Freund (New York: Harper and Row, 1969), 54–57.

2 Heidegger, *Contributions to Philosophy*, 11.

3 Heidegger, *Contributions to Philosophy*, 77. Heidegger's *Erschrecken* could easily be confused with Sartre's 'nausea', but as Charles E. Scott points out, Sartre's conception of our relation to being is so fundamentally different from Heidegger's as to rule this out: 'The problem with Sartre's description of nausea . . . is that he experiences things so much in terms of conscious autonomy and of consciousness' opposition to anything that is not conscious that he finds the borders of difference to constitute negation and something like death.' Scott, *The Lives of Things* (Bloomington: Indiana University Press, 2002), 30.

4 Heidegger, *Contributions to Philosophy*, 11.

⁵ See Scott, *The Lives of Things*, for a defence of the view that scientists, as scientists, can be filled with the same sort of wonder as poets, and that philosophers need not favour the latter over the former. I do not doubt that this is true, but nevertheless, science always presents the possibility of dismissive reduction, and even if we (the scientistic general public, as much as scientists in particular) do not *always* succumb to it, we very often do.

⁶ Plato, *Theaetetus*, Loeb Classical Library edn, tr. H. N. Fowler (Cambridge, MA: Harvard University Press, 1921), 155c–d.

⁷ Plato, *Theaetetus*, tr. F. M. Cornford, in Edith Hamilton and Huntington Cairns, eds, *Collected Dialogues of Plato* (Princeton: Princeton University Press, 1961).

⁸ This translation is Gail Fine's and T. H. Irwin's, in S. Marc Cohen et al., eds, *Readings in Ancient Greek Philosophy*, 690. The full sentence in the Greek is 'Πάντες ἄνθρωποι τοῦ εἰδέναι ὀρέγονται φύσει.' Aristotle, *Metaphysics*, Loeb Classical Library edn, tr. Hugh Tredennick with Greek original (Cambridge, MA: Harvard University Press, 1933), 980a22.

⁹ Aristotle, *Physics*, Loeb Classical Library edn, tr. Philip H. Wickstead and Francis M. Cornford with original Greek (Cambridge, MA: Harvard University Press, 1963), 184a10–16.

¹⁰ Aristotle, *Metaphysics*, 981a26–30.

¹¹ This might seem at odds with Aristotle's notion of 'contemplation', θεωρία, which he identifies as the source of the highest kind of happiness in the *Nicomachean Ethics*. Of this, Amélie Rorty comments: 'characterized by its attitude as well as by its objects, *theoria* is the self-contained activity par excellence.... When he contemplates the divine, or the fixed stars, the contemplator is no more interested in explaining them – no more interested in constructing the science of theology or astronomy – than he is in achieving nobility or serenity.' Rorty, 'The Place of Contemplation in Aristotle's *Nicomachean Ethics*', in *Essays on Aristotle's Ethics*, ed. Rorty (Berkeley: University of California Press, 1980), 378. If this is an accurate description of the activity of θεωρία, then θεωρία is not philosophy. Aristotle's own philosophical activity does not match this description; his works may counsel, but they do not consist in, this kind of self-contained contemplation.

¹² Heidegger, *What is Philosophy?*, 85.

¹³ Of course, this does not entail any 'ethical' condemnation of philosophy; in any event, as we saw in the Introduction, oblivion of being may allow for a deeper dwelling in our fitting together with being when we 'return home' to it.

¹⁴ Heidegger, *Being and Time*, 42.

¹⁵ Heidegger, 'Letter on "humanism" ', 156–157.

¹⁶ Heidegger, 'Letter on "humanism" ', 156.

¹⁷ Heidegger, *Being and Time*, 42.

¹⁸ Heidegger, *Being and Time*, 43.

¹⁹ Heidegger, *Being and Time*, 42.

²⁰ See, for example, Heidegger, *The Basic Problems of Phenomenology*, 267.

²¹ Heidegger explains the new sense he is trying to give to *Wesen* in a paragraph inserted into 'On the essence of truth' in 1949: 'The question of the essence of truth arises from the question of the truth of essence. In the former question essence is understood initially in the sense of whatness (*quidditas*) or material

content (*realitas*) . . . . In the question of the truth of essence, essence is understood verbally' – that is, as a verb; 'in this word, remaining still within metaphysical presentation, being [*Seyn*] is thought as the difference that holds sway between being and beings.' Heidegger, 'On the essence of truth', 96; GA 9, 96.

22 Heidegger, 'Letter on "humanism"', 153.
23 Heidegger, 'Letter on "humanism"', 148; GA 9, 148.
24 Heidegger, 'On the question of being', 236; GA 9, 236.
25 Heidegger, 'The principle of identity', 31/94.
26 Heidegger, 'Letter on "humanism"', 188; GA 9, 188.
27 Heidegger, *Contributions to Philosophy*, 330; GA 65, 470.
28 Heidegger, 'Letter on "humanism"', 192; GA 9, 192. Capuzzi has 'clearing' for *lichtend*, in keeping with the accepted translation of *Lichtung*, but 'lighting' seems to make more sense in this context.
29 Heidegger, 'The turning', 38–39; GA 79, 69.
30 On the 'captivation' of non-human animals, see Heidegger, *The Fundamental Concepts of Metaphysics*, 236–267.
31 Heidegger, 'Letter on "humanism"', 165.
32 Heidegger, 'What is metaphysics?', in *Pathmarks*, ed. William McNeill (New York: Cambridge University Press, 1998).
33 Heidegger, 'Letter on "humanism"', 165.
34 Heidegger, *Contributions to Philosophy*, 179; GA 65, 254. 'Being' translates *Seyn* throughout this passage.
35 Heidegger, 'Letter on "humanism"', 163.
36 Heidegger, 'On the question of being', 236–237; GA 9, 236–237.
37 Heidegger, 'The principle of identity', 27.
38 Heidegger, 'On the question of being', 235; GA 9, 235.
39 Heidegger, 'Time and being', 12.
40 Heidegger, 'On the question of being', 239.
41 Heidegger, 'On the question of being', 239.
42 The current convention, following Hofstadter, is to translate both terms with 'the fourfold', but I think 'gathered four' captures the sense of the prefix *Ge-*, which is important in Heidegger's conception of the thing as a gatherer, and 'fouring' helps capture the sense that the thing's gathering is a happening.
43 Heidegger, 'The thing', 178; GA 79, 17–18. Note that the *Gesamtausgabe* text, which I follow here, differs from that published in *Vorträge und Aufsätze*. In the former, the final phrase reads: '*nämlich als das Sein selbst*'; in the latter, which is translated in *Poetry, Language, Thought*, it reads: '*sogar als das Geheimnis des Seins selbst.*' *Vorträge und Aufsätze, Teil 2*, 51.
44 Heidegger, 'The thing', 178.
45 Heidegger, 'The thing', 178.
46 Heidegger, *Vorträge und Aufsätze, Teil 2*, 51; Heidegger, 'The thing', 178. Hofstadter has 'out of the hidden sway of the divinities' in the second sentence, but this is an error.
47 Heidegger, *Vorträge und Aufsätze, Teil 2*, 25; Heidegger, 'Building dwelling thinking', 150.
48 Heidegger, 'The thing', 178; GA 79, 17.

[49] Harper, *The Online Etymological Dictionary*, http://www.etymonline.com/index.
php?term=godhead and http://www.etymonline.com/index.php?term=-hood.

[50] Heidegger, *Parmenides*, 102–109.

[51] Heidegger, 'The thing', 178; GA 79, 17. Hofstadter mistakenly has 'divinities' for
'godhead' here; the translation of the corresponding passage in 'Building dwelling thinking' – which is identical at least this far – is correct. See Heidegger,
'Building dwelling thinking', 150; *Vorträge und Aufsätze, Teil 2*, 51.

[52] Heidegger, 'As When On a Holiday . . .', in *Elucidations of Hölderlin's Poetry*, tr.
Keith Hoeller (New York: Humanity Books, 2000), 89.

[53] Heidegger, 'The thing', 172–173; GA 79, 11–12.

[54] Heidegger, 'The thing', 173.

[55] Isak Dinesen, 'Babette's feast', in *Anecdotes of Destiny* (London: Penguin, 1986), 42.

[56] Dinesen, 'Babette's feast', 26.

[57] Dinesen, 'Babette's feast', 31.

[58] Dinesen, 'Babette's feast', 34.

[59] Dinesen, 'Babette's feast', 47.

[60] Dinesen, 'Babette's feast', 55.

[61] Heidegger, 'The thing', 172; *Vorträge und Aufsätze, Teil 2*, 45.

[62] Heidegger, 'The thing', 173.

[63] Dinesen, 'Babette's feast', 59.

[64] Dinesen, 'Babette's feast', 63.

[65] Dinesen, 'Babette's feast', 62.

[66] Dinesen, 'Babette's feast', 58.

[67] Dinesen, 'Babette's feast', 62.

[68] Dinesen, 'Babette's feast', 58.

[69] Dinesen, 'Babette's feast', 63.

[70] Heidegger, 'The thing', 165–166.

[71] Heidegger, 'The thing', 165.

[72] Heidegger, 'The thing', 166.

[73] Heidegger, 'Conversation on a country path about thinking', in Heidegger, *Discourse on Thinking*, tr. John M. Anderson and E. Hans Freund (New York: Harper
and Row, 1969), 89.

[74] Heidegger, 'The onto-theo-logical constitution of metaphysics', 64/132.

[75] See the photograph found on the National Gallery of Canada's website: http://
cybermuse.gallery.ca/cybermuse/search/artwork_e.jsp?mkey=35828 (accessed
on 6 November 2008).

[76] At least, there should be no question. As a matter of fact, however, if one spends
long enough in the vicinity of the *Voice of Fire*, one will inevitably hear people
discussing what they see in the painting.

[77] *The Online Etymological Dictionary*, http://www.etymonline.com/index.php?
term=reverence

[78] Heidegger, 'As When On a Holiday . . .', 89.

[79] Notice that, assuming gods are conscious, things already are for a creator god
before creation, even if those things are only ideas.

[80] For Moore's open question argument, see G. E. Moore, *Principia Ethica* (New
York: Cambridge University Press, 1993), §§12–14.

[81] Vladimir Nabokov, *Pale Fire* (New York: Vintage, 1989), p. 13.

Chapter 4

1 Heidegger, 'Time and being', 6; GA 14, 10. In 'Time and being', Heidegger indicates the relationship between being in the sense of its epochal destinings and being in the sense of *Ereignis*, but in this lecture he almost solely reserves the word *Sein* for the first sense.

2 *Oxford English Dictionary*, 2nd edn, s.v. 'present'.

3 Heidegger, 'Time and being', 9; GA 14, 13.

4 Heidegger, 'Time and being', 9; GA 14, 13.

5 Elements of it are laid out variously in such texts as the *Contributions to Philosophy*, especially 120, *The End of Metaphysics*, the *Nietzsche* lectures, and *The Principle of Reason*, tr. Reginald Lilly (Bloomington: Indiana University Press, 1996), as well as 'Time and being'.

6 Heidegger, 'Time and being', 9.

7 Heidegger, 'Time and being', 9; GA 14, 13.

8 Heidegger, *Nietzsche, Volume IV: Nihilism*, ed. David Farrell Krell, tr. Frank A. Capuzzi (New York: HarperCollins, 1982).

9 See, for example, Heidegger, *Contributions to Philosophy*, 120.

10 Heidegger, *Being and Time*, 2.

11 Heidegger, *An Introduction to Metaphysics*, 15.

12 Heidegger, *An Introduction to Metaphysics*, 30.

13 Heidegger, *Being and Time*, 176.

14 Heidegger, *Contributions to Philosophy*, 80; GA 65, 114.

15 Heidegger, 'On the question of being', 314.

16 Heidegger, *Contributions to Philosophy*, 77.

17 Heidegger, *Contributions to Philosophy*, 78.

18 Heidegger, 'On the question of being', 243.

19 Heidegger, 'The thing', 168; GA 79, 7.

20 Heidegger, 'On the question of being', 243. When Heidegger says that the Greeks experienced the oblivion of being, clearly what he means is not that they experienced that oblivion as oblivion – to experience oblivion as oblivion is already to have begun overcoming it – but rather that their experience underwent that oblivion.

21 Heidegger, 'The thing', 165.

22 Heidegger, 'The thing', 165.

23 Heidegger, 'The thing', 166.

24 Heidegger, 'The thing', 178.

25 Heidegger, 'The question concerning technology', in *The Question Concerning Technology and Other Essays*, tr. William Lovitt (New York: Harper Torchbooks, 1977), 17. See also Heidegger, 'What are poets for?', in *Poetry, Language Thought*, tr. Albert Hofstadter (New York: Harper & Row, 1975), 113, for the connection between Nietzsche and technologism.

26 Heidegger, 'The question concerning technology', 16.

27 See *Nietzsche, Volume I: The Will to Power as Art*, ed. and tr. David Farrell Krell (New York: HarperCollins, 1991) for Heidegger's critique of aesthetics along these lines.

28 Heidegger, 'The question concerning technology', 14.

29 Heidegger, 'The question concerning technology', 27.
30 Heidegger, 'The question concerning technology', 28; Heidegger, *Die Technik und die Kehre* (Tübingen: Neske, 1962), 27.
31 Heidegger, 'The way to language', 131–132; GA 12, 251.
32 *German Dictionary Plus Grammar* (Glasgow: HarperCollins, 1998), s.v. *verstellen*.
33 See Heidegger, *Nietzsche IV*, 123–138.
34 Nietzsche, *Thus Spoke Zarathustra*, in *The Portable Nietzsche*, ed. and tr. Walter Kaufmann (New York: Penguin, 1976), 129.
35 Nietzsche, *Thus Spoke Zarathustra*, 129.
36 Heidegger, 'Only a god can save us', 277.
37 Heidegger, *An Introduction to Metaphysics*, 11.
38 Heidegger, *An Introduction to Metaphysics*, 14; GA 40, 13.
39 Heidegger, *An Introduction to Metaphysics*, 11.
40 See *The Online Etymological Dictionary*, http://www.etymonline.com/index.php?term=be, http://www.etymonline.com/index.php?term=boast, and http://www.etymonline.com/index.php?term=bucket.
41 Heidegger, *An Introduction to Metaphysics*, 59; GA 40, 54.
42 Heidegger, *An Introduction to Metaphysics*, 12; GA 40, 16–17.
43 Heidegger, '*Aletheia* (Heraclitus, fragment B 16)', in *Early Greek Thinking*, tr. David Farrell Krell and Frank A. Capuzzi (New York: Harper & Row, 1975), 114; Heidegger, *Vorträge und Aufsätze, Teil 3*, (Tübingen: Gunther Neske Pfullingen, 1967), 67.
44 Heidegger, *An Introduction to Metaphysics*, 50; GA 40, 46–47.
45 Heidegger, *Being and Time*, 25.
46 Heidegger, *An Introduction to Metaphysics*, 11; GA 40, 11.
47 Heidegger, *An Introduction to Metaphysics*, 1; GA 40, 1.
48 Heidegger, *Nietzsche I*, 48.

Conclusion

1 Searle writes that 'we have now, at least, cleared away [some] of the worst mistakes in dealing with the subject [of consciousness], beginning with the view that consciousness does not exist at all, that it is just an illusion, and there really are not subjective, qualitative states of sentience and awareness'. Searle, 'Consciousness: What we still don't know', *The New York Review of Books* 52, no. 1 (2005): 36–39, 39. But while it may be the case generally that computationalism and other varieties of eliminativism have fallen out of fashion among philosophers of mind and cognitive scientists, my experience is that they are still very popular among educated laypeople, who tend to view them as the only alternatives to religiously founded forms of substance dualism. My experience is also that while cognitive scientists, whether they are housed in philosophy or psychology departments, now speak easily of consciousness, what they mean by 'consciousness' often seems to be nothing more than a physical activity centred in the brain, not clearly distinguishable from the 'consciousness' that one might attribute to an information processing machine. I suspect that their understanding of Searle's slogan 'the mind is what the brain does' is very different from Searle's own.

Bibliography

Ackrill, J. L. 'Aristotle on *eudaimonia*'. In *Essays on Aristotle's Ethics*. Ed. Amélie Oksenberg Rorty. Berkeley: University of California Press, 1980.

Annas, Julia. 'Happiness as achievement'. *Daedalus* 133, no. 2 (Spring 2004): 44–51.

Annas, Julia. *The Morality of Happiness*. New York: Oxford University Press, 1993.

Aristotle. *Metaphysics*. Loeb Classical Library edn. Tr. Hugh Tredennick with Greek original. Cambridge, MA: Harvard University Press, 1933.

Aristotle. *Nicomachean Ethics*. Loeb Classical Library edn. Tr. H. Rackham with Greek original. Cambridge, MA: Harvard University Press, 1962.

Aristotle. *Physics*. Loeb Classical Library edn. Tr. Philip H. Wickstead and Francis M. Cornford with Greek original. Cambridge, MA: Harvard University Press, 1963.

Aurelius Antoninus, Marcus. *The Communings with Himself of Marcus Aurelius Antoninus*. Loeb Classical Library edn. Tr. C. R. Haines with Greek original. Cambridge, MA: Harvard University Press, 1961.

Austin, J. L. *How to Do Things with Words*. Ed. J. O. Urmson and Marina Sbisà. Oxford: Clarendon Press, 1975.

Bentham, Jeremy. *Deontology, Together with a Table of the Springs of Action and Articles on Utilitarianism*. In *Collected Works of Jeremy Bentham*. Ed. Amnon Goldworth. New York: Oxford University Press, 1983.

Bentham, Jeremy. *Introduction to the Principles of Morals and Legislation*. Ed. J. H. Burns and H. L. A. Hart. London: Athlone Press, 1970.

Boss, Medard. 'Martin Heidegger's Zollikon Seminars'. Tr. Brian Kenny. *Review of Existential Psychology and Psychiatry* 16 (1979): 7–20.

Butler, James. 'The arguments for the most pleasant life in *Republic* IX'. *Apeiron* 32 (1999): 37–48.

Carman, Taylor. *Heidegger's Analytic: Interpretation, Discourse, and Authenticity in Being and Time*. New York: Cambridge University Press, 2003.

Claiborne, Robert, ed. *Roots of English*. New York: TimesBooks, 1978.

Cohen, S. Marc, Patricia Curd and C. D. C. Reeve, eds. *Readings in Ancient Greek Philosophy From Thales to Aristotle*. 2nd edn. Indianapolis: Hackett Publishing Company, 2000.

Crowell, Steven Galt. 'Metaphysics, metontology, and the end of *Being and Time*'. In *Heidegger Reexamined, Volume I: Dasein, Authenticity, and Death*. Eds Hubert L. Dreyfus and Mark Wrathall. New York: Routledge, 2002.

Davis, Wayne. 'A theory of happiness', *The American Philosophical Quarterly* 18, no. 2 (April 1981): 111–120.

De Heer, C. *Makar–Eudaimon–Olbios–Eutuchis: A Study of the Semantic Field Denoting Happiness in Ancient Greek to the End of the 5th Century B.C.* Amsterdam: Adolf M. Hakkert, 1969.

Den Uyl, Douglas and Tibor R. Machan. 'Recent work on the concept of happiness'. *American Philosophical Quarterly* 20, no. 2 (April 1983): 115–134.

Derrida, Jacques. *Speech and Phenomena and Other Essays on Husserl's Theory of Signs.* Tr. David B. Allison. Evanston, IL: Northwestern University Press, 1973.

Destrée, Pierre and Nicholas D. Smith, eds. *Socrates' Divine Sign: Religion, Practice, and Value in Socratic Philosophy.* Kelowna, BC: Academic Printing and Publishing, 2005.

Dinesen, Isak. 'Babette's feast'. In Dinesen, *Anecdotes of Destiny.* London: Penguin, 1986.

Dreyfus, Hubert L. *Being-in-the-World: A Commentary on Heidegger's* Being and Time, *Division I.* Cambridge, MA: MIT Press, 1991.

Dreyfus, Hubert and John Haugeland. 'Husserl and Heidegger: Philosophy's last stand'. In *Heidegger and Modern Philosophy.* Ed. Michael Murray. New Haven: Yale University Press, 1978.

Foucault, Michel. 'Nietzsche, genealogy, history'. In *Essential Works of Foucault, 1954–1984, Volume Two: Aesthetics, Method, and Epistemology.* Ed. James D. Faubion. Tr. Donald F. Bouchard and Sherry Simon. New York: The New Press, 1998.

Friedman, Michael. *A Parting of the Ways: Carnap, Cassirer, Heidegger.* Chicago: Open Court, 2000.

Frost, Robert. 'The tuft of flowers'. In *The Poetry of Robert Frost: The Collected Poems, Complete and Unabridged.* Ed. Edward Connery Lathem. New York: Henry Holt and Company, 1979.

German Dictionary Plus Grammar. Glasgow: HarperCollins, 1998.

Harper, Douglas, ed. *The Online Etymological Dictionary.* http://www.etymonline.com/

Haybron, Daniel M. 'Two philosophical problems in the study of happiness'. *Journal of Happiness Studies* 1 (2000): 207–225.

Haybron, Daniel M. 'What do we want from a theory of happiness?'. *Metaphilosophy* 34, no. 3 (April 2003): 305–328.

Heidegger, Martin. '*Aletheia* (Heraclitus, fragment B 16)'. In *Early Greek Thinking.* Tr. David Farrell Krell and Frank A. Capuzzi. New York: Harper and Row, 1975.

Heidegger, Martin. 'The Anaximander Fragment'. In *Early Greek Thinking.* Tr. David Farrell Krell and Frank A. Capuzzi. New York: Harper and Row, 1984.

Heidegger, Martin. 'Anaximander's Saying'. In *Off the Beaten Track.* Ed. and tr. Julian Young and Kenneth Haynes. New York: Cambridge University Press, 2002.

Heidegger, Martin. 'As When on a Holiday . . .'. In *Elucidations of Hölderlin's Poetry.* Tr. Keith Hoeller. New York: Humanity Books, 2000.

Heidegger, Martin. *Basic Concepts.* Tr. Gary E. Aylesworth. Bloomington: Indiana University Press, 1993.

Heidegger, Martin. *The Basic Problems of Phenomenology.* Tr. Albert Hofstadter. Bloomington: Indiana University Press, 1988.

Heidegger, Martin. *Being and Time.* Tr. John Macquarrie and Edward Robinson. New York: Harper and Row, 1962.

Heidegger, Martin. *Being and Time.* Tr. Joan Stambaugh. Albany: State University of New York Press, 1996.

Heidegger, Martin. 'Building dwelling thinking'. In *Poetry, Language, Thought*. Tr. Albert Hofstadter. New York: Harper and Row, 1975.

Heidegger, Martin. *Contributions to Philosophy (From Enowning)*. Tr. Parvis Emad and Kenneth Maly. Bloomington: Indiana University Press, 1999.

Heidegger, Martin 'Conversation on a country path about thinking'. In *Discourse on Thinking*. Tr. John M. Anderson and E. Hans Freund. New York: Harper and Row, 1969.

Heidegger, Martin. 'A dialogue on language'. In *On the Way to Language*. Tr. Peter D. Hertz. New York: HarperCollins, 1982.

Heidegger, Martin. *Four Seminars*. Tr. Andrew Mitchell and François Raffoul. Bloomington: Indiana University Press, 2003.

Heidegger, Martin. *The Fundamental Concepts of Metaphysics: World, Finitude, Solitude*. Tr. William McNeill and Nicholas Walker. Bloomington: Indiana University Press, 1995.

Heidegger, Martin. *Gesamtausgabe*. Ed. Friedrich-Wilhelm von Herrmann et al. Frankfurt am Main: Vittorio Klostermann, 1975–2005.

Heidegger, Martin. *Hölderlin's Hymn 'The Ister'*. Tr. William McNeill and Julia Davis. Bloomington: Indiana University Press, 1996.

Heidegger, Martin. *An Introduction to Metaphysics*. Tr. Ralph Manheim. New York: Anchor Books, 1961.

Heidegger, Martin. 'Language'. In *Poetry, Language, Thought*. Tr. Albert Hofstadter. New York: Harper and Row, 1975.

Heidegger, Martin. 'Letter on "humanism"'. In *Pathmarks*. Ed. William McNeill. New York: Cambridge University Press, 1998.

Heidegger, Martin. 'Memorial address'. In *Discourse on Thinking*. Tr. John M. Anderson and E. Hans Freund. New York: Harper and Row, 1969.

Heidegger, Martin. *The Metaphysical Foundations of Logic*. Tr. Michael Heim. Bloomington: Indiana University Press, 1984.

Heidegger, Martin. 'Metaphysics as history of being: Whatness and thatness in the essential beginning of metaphysics'. In *The End of Philosophy*. Tr. Joan Stambaugh. Chicago: Chicago University Press, 2003.

Heidegger, Martin. 'My way to phenomenology'. In *On Time and Being*. Tr. Joan Stambaugh. Chicago: University of Chicago Press, 2002.

Heidegger, Martin. 'The nature of language'. In *On the Way to Language*. Tr. Peter D. Hertz. New York: HarperCollins, 1982.

Heidegger, Martin. *Nietzsche, Erster Band*. Tübingen: Verlag Günther Neske Pfullingen, 1961.

Heidegger, Martin. *Nietzsche, Volume I: The Will to Power as Art*. Ed. and tr. David Farrell Krell. New York: HarperCollins, 1991.

Heidegger, Martin. *Nietzsche, Volume II: The Eternal Recurrence of the Same*. Ed. and tr. David Farrell Krell. New York: HarperCollins, 1991.

Heidegger, Martin. *Nietzsche, Volume III: The Will to Power as Knowledge and as Metaphysics*. Ed. David Farrell Krell. Tr. Joan Stambaugh, David Farrell Krell and Frank A. Capuzzi. New York: HarperCollins, 1991.

Heidegger, Martin. *Nietzsche, Volume IV: Nihilism*. Ed. David Farrell Krell. Tr. Frank A. Capuzzi. New York: HarperCollins, 1991.

Heidegger, Martin. 'On the essence of ground'. In *Pathmarks*. Ed. William McNeill. New York: Cambridge University Press, 1998.

Heidegger, Martin. 'On the essence of truth'. In *Pathmarks*. Ed. William McNeill. New York: Cambridge University Press, 1998.

Heidegger, Martin. 'On the question of being'. In *Pathmarks*. Ed. William McNeill. New York: Cambridge University Press, 1998.

Heidegger, Martin. 'Only a god can save us: *Der Spiegel*'s interview with Martin Heidegger'. Tr. Maria P. Alter and John D. Caputo. *Philosophy Today* 20 (1976), 267–285.

Heidegger, Martin. 'The onto-theo-logical constitution of metaphysics'. In *Identity and Difference*. Tr. Joan Stambaugh with original German. Chicago: University of Chicago Press, 2002.

Heidegger, Martin. 'Overcoming metaphysics'. In *The End of Philosophy*. Tr. Joan Stambaugh. Chicago: Chicago University Press, 2003.

Heidegger, Martin. *Parmenides*. Tr. André Schuwer and Richard Rojcewicz. Bloomington: Indiana University Press, 1992.

Heidegger, Martin. 'The principle of identity'. In *Identity and Difference*. Tr. Joan Stambaugh with original German. Chicago: University of Chicago Press, 2002.

Heidegger, Martin. *The Principle of Reason*. Tr. Reginald Lilly. Bloomington: Indiana University Press, 1996.

Heidegger, Martin. 'The question concerning technology'. In *The Question Concerning Technology and Other Essays*. Tr. William Lovitt. New York: Harper Torchbooks, 1977.

Heidegger, Martin. *Die Technik und die Kehre*. Tübingen: Neske, 1962.

Heidegger, Martin. 'The thing'. In *Poetry, Language, Thought*. Tr. Albert Hofstadter. New York: Harper and Row, 1975.

Heidegger, Martin. 'The turning'. In *The Question Concerning Technology and Other Essays*. Tr. William Lovitt. New York: Harper Torchbooks, 1977.

Heidegger, Martin. 'Time and being'. In *On Time and Being*. Tr. Joan Stambaugh. Chicago: University of Chicago Press, 2002.

Heidegger, Martin. *Vorträge und Aufsätze, Teil 2*. Tübingen: Günther Neske Pfullingen, 1967.

Heidegger, Martin. *Vorträge und Aufsätze, Teil 3*. Tübingen: Günther Neske Pfullingen, 1967.

Heidegger, Martin. 'The way to language'. In *On the Way to Language*. Tr. Peter D. Hertz. New York: HarperCollins, 1982.

Heidegger, Martin. 'What are poets for?' In *Poetry, Language, Thought*. Tr. Albert Hofstadter. New York: Harper and Row, 1975.

Heidegger, Martin. *What is Called Thinking?*. Tr. J. Glenn Gray. New York: Harper and Row, 1968.

Heidegger, Martin. 'What is metaphysics?'. In *Pathmarks*. Ed. William McNeill. New York: Cambridge University Press, 1998.

Heidegger, Martin. *What is Philosophy?*. Tr. William Kluback and Jean T. Wilde with original German. New York: Twayne Publishers, 1958.

Heidegger, Martin. 'The word of Nietzsche: "God is dead"'. In *The Question Concerning Technology and Other Essays*. Tr. William Lovitt. New York: Harper Torchbooks, 1977.

Heraclitus of Ephesus. *Fragments*. Tr. T. M. Robinson with Greek original. Toronto: University of Toronto Press, 1987.

Hobbes, Thomas. *Leviathan*. Ed. C. B. Macpherson. New York: Penguin, 1985.

Kenny, Anthony. 'Happiness'. *Proceedings of the Aristotelian Society* 66 (1966): 93–102.

King, Matthew. 'Heidegger's etymological method: Discovering being by recovering the richness of the word', *Philosophy Today* 51, no. 3 (2007): 278–289.

Klein, Ernest. *A Comprehensive Etymological Dictionary of the English Language*. Amsterdam: Elsevier, 1966.

Kraut, Richard. 'Two conceptions of happiness'. *Philosophical Review* 88, no. 2 (April 1979): 167–197.

Krell, David Farrell. *Daimon Life*. Bloomington: Indiana University Press, 1992.

Krell, David Farrell. *Intimations of Mortality*. University Park, PA: Pennsylvania State University Press, 1986.

Liddell, H. G. and R. Scott, eds. *Greek-English Lexicon*. New York: Oxford University Press, 1996.

Locke, John. *Essay Concerning Human Understanding*. Oxford: Clarendon Press, 1956.

Mill, John Stuart. *Utilitarianism*. Toronto: Broadview Press, 2000.

Montague, Roger. 'Happiness'. *Proceedings of the Aristotelian Society* 67 (1967): 87–102.

Moore, G. E. *Principia Ethica*. New York: Cambridge University Press, 1993.

Morwood, James and John Taylor, eds. *Pocket Oxford Classical Greek Dictionary*. New York: Oxford University Press, 2002.

Nabokov, Vladimir. *Pale Fire*. New York: Vintage, 1989.

Nietzsche, Friedrich. *Thus Spoke Zarathustra*. In *The Portable Nietzsche*. Ed. and tr. Walter Kaufmann. New York: Penguin, 1976.

Nozick, Robert. *The Examined Life: Philosophical Meditations*. New York: Simon and Schuster, 1989.

Onions, C. T., ed. *Oxford Dictionary of English Etymology*. Oxford: Clarendon, 1969.

Ostenfeld, Erik Nis. *'Eudaimonia* in Plato's *Republic'*. In *Essays on Plato's Republic*. Ed. Erik Nis Ostenfeld. Aarhus: Aarhus University Press, 1998.

Oxford English Dictionary, 2nd edn. New York: Oxford University Press, 1989.

Partridge, Eric. *Origins: A Short Etymological Dictionary of Modern English*. New York: Macmillan, 1966.

Plato. *Apology*. Loeb Classical Library edn. Tr. H. N. Fowler with Greek original. Cambridge, MA: Harvard University Press, 1914.

Plato. *Meno*. Loeb Classical Library edn. Tr. W. R. M. Lamb with Greek original. Cambridge, MA: Harvard University Press, 1924.

Plato. *Phaedrus*. Loeb Classical Library edn. Tr. H. N. Fowler with Greek original. Cambridge, MA: Harvard University Press, 1914.

Plato. *Phaedrus*. Tr. R. Hackforth. In *Collected Dialogues*. Ed. Edith Hamilton. Princeton: Princeton University Press, 1961.

Plato. *Republic*. Loeb Classical Library edn. Tr. Paul Shorey with Greek original. Cambridge, MA: Harvard University Press, 1937.

Plato. *Symposium*. Loeb Classical Library ed. Tr. H. N. Fowler with Greek original. Cambridge, MA: Harvard University Press, 1914.

Plato. *Theaetetus*. Loeb Classical Library ed. Tr. H. N. Fowler with Greek original. Cambridge, MA: Harvard University Press, 1921.

Plato. *Theaetetus.* Tr. F. M. Cornford. In *Collected Dialogues of Plato.* Eds Edith Hamilton and Huntington Cairns. Princeton: Princeton University Press, 1961.

Plato. *Timaeus.* Loeb Classical Library edn. Tr. R. G. Bury with Greek original. Cambridge, MA: Harvard University Press, 1961.

Pöggeler, Otto. *Martin Heidegger's Path of Thinking.* Tr. Daniel Magurshak and Sigmund Barber. Atlantic Highlands, NJ: Humanities Press International, 1987.

Richardson, William J. *Heidegger: Through Phenomenology to Thought.* New York: Fordham University Press, 2003.

Rorty, Amélie Oksenberg. 'The place of contemplation in Aristotle's *Nicomachean Ethics*'. In *Essays on Aristotle's Ethics.* Ed. Amélie Oksenberg Rorty. Berkeley: University of California Press, 1980.

Scott, Charles E. *The Lives of Things.* Bloomington: Indiana University Press, 2002.

Schalow, Frank. 'Language and the etymological turn of thought'. *Graduate Faculty Philosophy Journal* 18, no. 1 (1995): 187–203.

Searle, John R. 'Consciousness: What we still don't know'. *The New York Review of Books* 52, no. 1 (2005): 36–39.

Searle, John R. 'Minds, brains, and programs'. In *The Nature of Mind.* Ed. David M. Rosenthal. New York: Oxford University Press, 1991.

Sheehan, Thomas. 'A paradigm shift in Heidegger research'. *Continental Philosophy Review* 32, no. 2 (2001): 1–20.

Smart, Ninian. 'What is happiness?'. In *The Good Life and its Pursuit.* Ed. Jude P. Dougherty. New York: Paragon House, 1984.

Sumner, L. W. 'Happiness now and then'. *Apeiron* 35, no. 4 (December 2002): 21–39.

Sumner, L. W. *Welfare, Happiness, and Ethics.* New York: Clarendon Press, 1996.

Tatarkiewicz, Wladyslaw. *Analysis of Happiness.* Tr. Edward Rothert and Danuta Zielinskn. The Hague: Martinus Nijhoff, 1976.

Vlastos, Gregory. 'Justice and happiness in the *Republic*'. In *Plato: A Collection of Critical Essays.* Ed. Gregory Vlastos. Vol. 2: *Ethics, Politics, and Philosophy of Art and Religion.* Garden City, NY: Anchor, 1971.

Wilson, John. 'Happiness'. *Analysis* 29 (1968): 13–21.

Zimmerman, Michael. *Eclipse of the Self: The Development of Heidegger's Concept of Authenticity.* Athens, OH: Ohio University Press, 1981.

Index

37267858R00085

Printed in Great Britain
by Amazon